SHE TOOK A VILLAGE

Other books by Alan Gottlieb

Politically Correct Guns
The Gun Grabbers
Alan Gottlieb's Celebrity Address Book
Gun Owner's Political Action Manual
Gun Rights Fact Book
The Rights of Gun Owners

With Dave Kopel:
Things You Can Do To Defend Your Gun Rights
More Things You Can Do To Defend Your Gun Rights

With George Flynn:
Guns for Women

With Ron Arnold:
Trashing the Economy
Politically Correct Environment

Edited:
The Wise Use Agenda
Fear of Food

SHE TOOK A VILLAGE

The Unauthorized Biography
of Hillary Rodham Clinton

Alan Gottlieb

Merril Press
Bellevue, Washington

SHE TOOK A VILLAGE

Typeset in Palatino by Merril Press, Bellevue, Washington. Cover design by Northwoods Studio. Cover photo by Doug Mills. Used with permission. Photo copyright © 1993 by AP/Wide World Photos. All rights reserved.

This book distributed by Merril Press, P.O. Box 1682, Bellevue, Washington 98009. Additional copies of this book may be ordered from Merril Press at $14.95 each. Phone 425-454-7009.

LIBRARY OF CONGRESS CATALOGING-IN-PUBLICATION DATA
Gottlieb, Alan M.
        She took a village : the unauthorized biography of Hillary Rodham Clinton / Alan Gottlieb.
                p.   cm.
        Includes bibliographical references and index.
        ISBN 0-936783-19-2 (pbk.)
        1. Clinton, Hillary Rodham. 2. Presidents' spouses — United States — Biography. I. Title.
E887.G68   1998
973.929'092 -- dc21
[B]   98-16324
                                                        CIP

Table of Contents

To my children,
Amy Jean, Sarah Merril, Alexis Hope
and Andrew Michael.
It doesn't take a village to raise them.

Introduction

Imagine. You hold the ultimate position of power. You were not hired, so you cannot be fired. You were not elected, so you cannot be impeached. You can select top officials or "ask" them to resign at will. Better yet, you can get your friends to do your dirty work for you. You don't have to conform to well-established methods of political conduct. You are completely unaccountable. You are First Lady of the United States of America.

Hillary Clinton has completely re-tailored this position to achieve such powerful heights. She has created for herself a completely unfettered realm in which to further her own particular political agendas. As the President's chief political and policy advisor, Hillary has become by far the most controversial First Lady in American history.

As the first of the First Ladies to come from the baby-boom generation, Hillary brings a new perspective to the position. Even such influential first ladies as Eleanor Roosevelt did not wield the kind of power that Hillary has found. Throughout her political career with Bill Clinton, Hillary has tried to soften her public image for the press to assuage the predominant old values about women's roles. Yet, she is well-educated, bright and articulate. She has always been the major bread-winner in the family with a very prominent career in law. While it may appear that she is hiding behind her husband's position, the truth is that she may very well be the first woman president of this country. And she faces zero accountability.

In researching this book, it became highly tempting to write it in a two-column format: one column titled "What They Said" and one titled "What They Did." I didn't need to: the Clintons' political oxymorons are outrageously clear. "Slick Willie" and "Slippery Hillary" are a mass of amusing —and sometimes frightening—contradictions.

Hillary's heart-warming book, *It Takes a Village*, titled after an African folk-saying, "It takes a village to raise a child," distracts the public with her concern for America's youth. Hillary puts on her maternal hat, trying to tell us how to raise our children. One can't help thinking of the old proverb, "the hand that rocks the cradle rules the world."

Of course, it may be a bit difficult to decipher just which parts of her book she actually believes in. Or her ghostwriter, Barbara Feinman, who, according to the *Washington Post*, received $120,000 from publisher Simon & Schuster for her services. Under the law, that's a gift to the *author* from the publisher—because ghost fees come from the *author*'s pocket, **not** the publisher's! Federal law says no government employee may accept such gifts. The Clinton administration has already argued, and the U.S. Court of Appeals agreed, that for purposes of one specific law—the Federal Advisory Committee Act—the first lady *is* a federal employee. When it comes to a gift from her publisher, it will be amusing to see if the Justice Department argues that Mrs. Clinton is not, after all, a federal employee.

In her quest for power, Hillary not only took the village—she took the entire country for a ride we will all be reeling from long after President Clinton's second term expires.

Alan Gottlieb
Liberty Park

1

Who is Hillary Clinton?

From the start, Hillary Clinton led what people in the '90s would consider a charmed life. Certainly not a child that had to be raised by the village, Hillary enjoyed the benefits of a two-parent household, with a hard-working father and a stay-at-home mother. A precocious child, she was always encouraged to excel, be it at academics, baseball or standing up to the neighborhood bully.

She was born Hillary Diane Rodham on October 26, 1947 at Edgewater Hospital in Chicago. Her mother chose the name Hillary because it sounded exotic—and daring, since Hillary was a boy's name at the time. According to her mother, Hillary was "a good-natured, nice little baby. She liked to have books read to her and she liked figuring out problems by herself. She was never shy and wasn't afraid of people or dogs or anything. When she was old enough to play outdoors by herself, she could beat up on the neighbors' children, but only if she had to. When she did, she'd go out, arms flailing, eyes closed—and whap! She'd get the better of them."

Her father, Hugh Ellsworth Rodham, graduated from Pennsylvania State University during the Depression and served as a basic training instructor in the navy during the war. He worked in Pennsylvania coal mines until taking a job as a textile salesman with Columbia Lace Company in Chicago. There he met Dorothy Emma Howell, whom he married in 1942, after a long-distance exchange of letters and pictures during the war. After serving in World War II, Hugh started his own drapery manufacturing business, which he was able to turn into a profitable enterprise.

Born in Scranton, Pennsylvania, Hugh was a second generation English immigrant (his father was four years old when the family moved to the United States). He had two brothers. Attending Penn State on a football scholarship, Hugh also played end for the Nittany Lions. He joined the Delta Upsilon fraternity and graduated with a bachelor of science degree in physical education in 1935.

In contrast, Dorothy Howell's life had been far from easy. Her father was Welsh and her mother was Scottish, French and Native American. Her parents were teenagers when she was born. Later, she was sent to live with very rigid grandparents, whom she left at four-

Who is Hillary Clinton?

teen to be a nanny while finishing school. Although she had only a high school education, Dorothy had a passion for knowledge, which she later sated with extension courses. Both parents' desire for a good education for all of their children especially rubbed off on Hillary. As cited in her compendium of quotes, *The Unique Voice of Hillary Rodham Clinton*, Hillary said her parents, "told me it was my obligation to go to school, that I had an obligation to use my mind. They told me that an education would enable me to have a lot more opportunities in life, that if I went to school and took it seriously and studied hard, not only would I learn things and become interested in the world around me, but I would open up all kinds of doors to myself so that, when I was older, I would have some control over my environment."

Hugh Rodham was a gruff, macho character. Curmudgeonly and hard to please, he kept his money and his praise with a tight fist. Martha Sherrill of the *Washington Post* interviewed many of Hillary's friends and family for her extensive, three-part feature on Hillary that appeared around the time the Clintons took office. Hillary's brother, Tony Rodham remembers their father bringing him and his brother along to help their father at work, *sans* pay. "Are you kidding?" Tony said. "We'd get, like, an extra potato at dinner." Hugh liked to keep up an image, however. His family was always well-dressed, and when his business became successful, he always drove Cadillacs. He always voted Republican, paving the way for his up-and-coming Goldwater Girl.

A stern disciplinarian and a strong believer in the Protestant work ethic, Hugh expected excellence in everything his children did. Hillary was the one who most met his standards (but he would always expect even better from her). He wouldn't let her get away with achieving only in academics, however, and made her practice her softball game for hours when she faltered. Hugh Rodham, Jr. excelled athletically, and played football at Penn State, his father's alma mater. Tony, the youngest, was the "problem" child, who didn't finish his college education and couldn't keep a job for very long.

Hillary said this of her childhood: "My parents gave me my belief in working hard, doing well in school and not being limited by the fact that I was a little girl. It really was the classic parenting situation, where the mother is the encourager and helper, and the father brings news from the outside world. My father would come home and say, 'You did well, but could you do better? It's hard out there.' Encouragement was tempered with realism."

In his book, *Boy Clinton*, R. Emmett Tyrrell, Jr. relates the following story about Hugh's tough demeanor: "An exacting taskmaster for his three children, Father Rodham does not sound very agreeable. In adulthood his daughter would tell stories about his strict regimen. When she was Arkansas's First Lady, one of Chelsea's nannies overheard her lecturing her negligent daughter, telling her that back in Park Ridge she *always* had to replace the toothpaste cap. On one occasion when she failed, her father threw it out the window and sent her into the icy Midwestern morn to retrieve it."

Hugh had a softer side, too. He was very much a family man, moving to Little Rock with Dorothy after he had triple bypass heart surgery. There, they both spent much time babysitting granddaughter Chelsea. He even made an exception in the voting booth for his son-in-law, the first Democrat for whom he had ever voted.

In her book, *On the Make: The Rise of Bill Clinton*, Meredith L. Oakley, a reporter who spent 13 years following Bill Clinton's rise to fame, relates the following story about Hugh. "Public appearances were few and far between, even during the presidential campaign, although Hugh relented after the 1992 election when the Clintons' strongest Hollywood boosters, Harry Thomason and his wife Linda Bloodworth-Thomason [of the hit television sitcom, *Designing Women*], persuaded him to do a cameo on their newest situation comedy, 'Hearts Afire.' Seated in a high-backed chair, a frail-looking Hugh Rodham had one line in which he paid tribute to the two women dearest to him. Upon overhearing a conversation in which a senatorial aide, played by actor John Ritter, observes that Hillary Clinton is a 'fox,' Rodham barks, 'If you think she's a fox, you should see her mother!'"

Hugh died on April 7, 1993, from a stroke he had suffered three weeks earlier. He was eighty-two at the time. At his funeral, a navy honor guard carried his flag-draped casket. Ms.

Oakley writes, "Friends say Hugh's death was deeply felt by his only daughter, who had maintained a sixteen-day vigil at his bedside. Hillary had prepared for this moment, and took comfort in her religious faith, and she fully intended to be with him and the rest of the family when the end came, but she was not. During that period, she had canceled a string of public appearances, including the opening session of her newly formed national task force on health care reform, but three days before Hugh died, she had returned to her White House duties.

"Observers marveled at her composure upon returning to Arkansas to oversee funeral arrangements, and the calm demeanor she displayed throughout the services, but it was a painful undertaking. As Hugh, Jr., remarked during an interview several weeks before his father's death, 'She was a daddy's girl, there's no doubt about it.'"

Hillary's mother, Dorothy, provided a positive female role model, fulfilling the typical homemaker role of that era. Yet she expected Hillary to be as strong as any boy, and wouldn't let Hillary limit herself just because she was a girl. In an interview in the May 1992 edition of *Vanity Fair*, Dorothy said that "no daughter of mine was going to go through the agony of being afraid to say what she had on her mind." Certainly no one could accuse Hillary of that!

Her mother taught her other valuable lessons. In Hillary's words, "I would just add about my mother that she had a social conscience at a time when that was not even fashionable. She was always trying to make sure that we understood what was fair and what was just. She encouraged us to speak out and not worry about what anybody else thought, just to be ourselves."

Hillary's parents were crucial in instilling the overachiever mentality that carries over into her life today. Her mother encouraged her to stand up for herself, and her father insisted that no matter how good she did, she could always do better. She remembers, "I would come home from school with a good grade, and my father would say, 'Must have been an easy assignment.'"

When Hillary was three, she and her parents moved to Park Ridge, an upper middle-class suburb of Chicago, where she attended public schools with her two younger brothers. In their new locale, the Rodhams were a typical 1950s family, with her mother staying home and her father commuting to Chicago to run his business. They attended a local Methodist church, and the neighborhood was full of other children to play with.

According to her mother, "There must have been 40 or 50 children within a four-block radius of our house and within four years of Hillary's age. There were more boys than girls, lots of playing and competition. She held her own at cops and robbers, hide and seek, chase and run—all the games that children don't play anymore."

In her *Vanity Fair* interview, Dorothy recounted a story from when Hillary was four years old and in tears from yet another encounter with the neighborhood bully. Dorothy told her, "There's no room in this house for cowards. You're going to have to stand up to her. The next time she hits you, I want you to hit her back." Hillary dutifully obeyed, throwing the first punch the next time the bully came up to her, and enjoyed the fruits of this early assertiveness lesson by being allowed to play with the other children instead of crying on the sidelines.

A natural leader, Hillary thrived on organizing activities, including a neighborhood circus. Dorothy noted, "Mothers in the neighborhood were amazed at how they couldn't get their boys to do much, but Hillary had them all running around."

This natural charisma proved useful throughout her whole life. As Meredith Oakley relates in *On the Make*, "Boys were attracted by Hillary's personality and the ease with which she addressed them. Neither presumptuous nor flirtatious, she met them as equals, and they accepted that, apparently never realizing how much they acquiesced to do her bidding, whether undertaking a fund-raising event to benefit the migrant workers who worked on the nearby farms or organizing school assemblies for the 2,700-member Maine Township High School-South." In a 1992 interview with Gail Sheehy, Dorothy said, "Boys responded to Hillary. She just took charge, and they let her." These skills would come in handy later for running a nation!

"Sure, my sister is tough as nails," says brother Tony Rodham. "She's a lot of those things that people have said she was." Her other brother, Hugh, notes, "But that's just one facet. That's her business face. You know, like your game face when you play football?"

Even in elementary school, Hillary made high grades. She was known for being a chronic teacher's pet at Eugene Field Grammar School in Park Ridge and at Ralph Waldo Emerson Junior High. In Girl Scouts, she earned every possible merit badge. The only talents that didn't seem to come naturally to her were playing the piano and ballet dancing.

She was the perpetual do-gooder. On top of almost constant perfect grades, she never got in trouble or got detention. In high school, she refused to let her friends pierce her ears with a needle and potato, didn't smoke in the bathroom or make out with boys in "The Pit" at Maine South's library, and didn't even wear black turtlenecks. She never cut class, except, as good friend Betsy Johnson Ebeling remembers in Ms. Sherrill's feature in the *Washington Post*, "The only time I remember us doing that was Senior Ditch Day, kind of an organized event—and we thought we were being very daring."

A formative experience in Hillary's young life occurred in 1957, when she wrote a letter to NASA after the Soviet Union launched Sputnik. She wanted to find out how to best pursue a career as an astronaut. NASA replied that they were not accepting women as astronauts, which infuriated Hillary. Her mother had raised her to believe that success was not confined to men. "There was no distinction between me and my brother, or any barriers thrown up to me that I couldn't think about doing something because I was a girl," she remembers in Aaron Boyd's biography, *First Lady: The Story of Hillary Rodham Clinton*. "It was just: if you work hard enough and you really apply yourself, then you should be able to do whatever you choose to do."

At Maine Township High School-South, Hillary noticed that many of her female friends began holding themselves back so that boys would not be intimidated by them. She did not approve of them taking less demanding courses to be in the same classes as their boyfriends, and was determined that her social life would not interfere with her school work. Later on, she would compromise these very same beliefs for a certain young man from Arkansas.

Hillary immersed herself in extracurricular activities, organizing talent shows and school assemblies, and participating in school government as president of her junior class. As a member of the student council, she organized a mock political convention at her school. In Ms. Sherrill's article, Hillary's childhood friend, Rick Ricketts, recalls her organizational ability: "She even had political demonstrations planned in the aisles." She was a member of the National Honor Society and won the Good Citizen Award from the Daughters of the American Revolution. Her senior class voted her as "Most Likely To Succeed."

"There was a small group of us at Maine South, competing for the National Honor Society and other things. We all knew each other's

Who is Hillary Clinton?

grade point average," said Bob Stenson in an interview with Ms. Sherrill, a classmate of Hillary's who remembers graduating seventh out of 1,000 in the class of 1965, and Hillary being around 15th. "She was strong and secure and graceful—almost aloof. I always felt a little funny around her. She was a tough competitor and formidable. I was always hoping she'd stumble a little bit."

When her mother suggested Hillary should wear make-up, Hillary refused. "I think she thought (makeup) was superficial and silly," her mother said. "She didn't have time for it." One of her high school classmates, Jeannie Snodgrass Almo, told Ms. Sherrill, "She had absolutely no vanity. She was totally un-concerned about how she appeared to people— and she was loved for that." She preferred to think about and discuss politics, Sputnik and sports (she could spout off baseball stats with the best of them).

During her high school years, Hillary worked in a daycare center, then as a store clerk and had a summer job maintaining sports equipment in a park. In her senior year, after losing the bid to be president of her senior class, Hillary volunteered on Republican Barry Goldwater's presidential campaign, wearing a sash proclaiming "Goldwater Girl."

Sheltered by her Republican, upper-middle-class existence, Hillary was especially hit hard by the realities of life she would be exposed to through her church's youth group. Her family attended First United Methodist in a red brick church not far from their house.

JHE TOOK A VILLAGE

With other members of her youth group, Hillary worked with organizations helping the urban poor of Chicago. She organized volunteers to baby-sit the children of migrant workers.

During her high school years, under the mentorship of youth minister Donald Jones (no relation to Paula Jones of the sex scandal), Hillary's views began their slide to the left. Kids attending Don Jones' Thursday night classes called them "The University of Life." Jones introduced them to the world outside of their white-bread existence, discussing everything from Picasso's "Guernica" to Rod Serling's "Requiem for a Heavyweight."

Jones also took his class to Chicago's South Side, introducing the Park Ridge kids to street kids, gang members and the world of poor and working-class Hispanics and blacks. In Judith Warner's biography, *Hillary Clinton: The Inside Story*, Don Jones said, "I don't think those kids had ever seen poverty before. Religion, going to church, tended to function there for most people to reinforce their rather traditional conservative values, and so when I came in and took that white, middle-class youth group into the inner city of Chicago, that was quite radical." In 1962, he took them to Chicago's "Sunday Evening Club" to hear the Reverend Martin Luther King, Jr. speak. Hillary even got to shake his hand.

In the spring of her senior year, Hillary finally ventured out boy-hunting, and rented a station wagon with seven other girls during Easter break. They headed to Pompano Beach in Florida, inspired by the movie *Where the Boys*

Who is Hillary Clinton?

Are. "We thought we'd meet boys from all over the world," said Betsy Ebeling, who also made the trip. "But the first walk we took on the beach, we ran into three guys from Maine East and hung out with them the whole time."

Hillary has long been known for her loyalty to her friends and mentors, continuing personal contact with such people as Donald Jones and Marian Wright Edelman, the founder of Children's Defense Fund. She attends her high school reunions in Chicago, staying the night with friend Betsy Johnson Ebeling.

Martha Sherrill noted that many of Hillary's friends that she interviewed were visibly overcome with emotion when calling up memories of Hillary, and how "the world has so grossly misunderstood their warm, funny, smart, tough, loyal Hillary." Sherrill writes, "the Weepers [Hillary's friends]...describe a friend who never gripes, never self-obsesses, never discusses 'the pain' Bill Clinton caused in their marriage [i.e., the 'pains' like Gennifer Flowers, Paula Jones and Monica Lewinsky], and who has a belly laugh you can hear all across the governor's mansion. They describe a friend who never fails to ask what books they're reading, how their husbands are doing, knows where their children are going to school and what disease their parents are dying of."

JHE TOOK A VILLAGE
Notes on Chapter 1

Page 3. Osborne, Claire G., ed. *The Unique Voice of Hillary Rodham Clinton: A Portrait in Her Own Words,* New York: Avon Books, 1997.

Page 3. Sherrill, Martha. "Growing Up Hillary," Part two of three, *Washington Post*, January 20, 1993.

Page 4. Tyrrell, R. Emmett, Jr. *Boy Clinton: The Political Biography,* Washington, D.C.: Regnery Publishing, Inc., 1996.

Page 5. Oakley, Meredith L. *On the Make: The Rise of Bill Clinton,* Washington, D.C.: Regnery Publishing, 1994.

Page 6. *Vanity Fair*, May 1992.

Page 7. *Vanity Fair*, May 1992.

Page 8. Oakley, Meredith L. *On the Make.*

Page 8. Sheedy, Gail. Interview. 1992.

Page 9. Sherrill, Martha. "Growing Up Hillary," *Washington Post*, January 20, 1993.

Page 10. Boyd, Aaron. *First Lady: The Story of Hillary Rodham Clinton,* Greensboro: Morgan Reynolds, 1994.

Page 10. Sherrill, Martha. "Growing Up Hillary."

Page 11. Sherrill, Martha. "Growing Up Hillary."

Page 12. Warner, Judith. *Hillary Clinton: Inside Story.*

Page 13. Sherrill, Martha. "Growing Up Hillary."

2
Wellesley, Yale and Bill

From her sheltered life in suburban Chicago, Hillary moved on to Wellesley College, a prestigious women's college near Boston. A favorite teacher recommended this expensive school, which took the "liberal" in "liberal arts" very seriously. The students were the crème de la crème of the social and economic elite, and had the means to immerse themselves in the angst of the time. In an interview in the May 1992 edition of *Vanity Fair*, Hillary found these privileged environs "all very rich and fancy and very intimidating."

Here, Hillary met the daughters of many influential people. Her best friend there, Eldee Acheson, was the granddaughter of Dean

15

Acheson, Secretary of State under Truman. One acquaintance was the daughter of Paul Nitze, Deputy Secretary of Defense under Kennedy and Johnson, and later Chief Arms Negotiator for Reagan.

But it was the 1960s, when the trappings of the rich and famous were too conformist. In the spirit of the new radical environment, Hillary gave up her bobby socks and thick glasses in favor of John Lennon-type "granny glasses" and peasant dresses or jeans. During this time, Hillary's political beliefs shifted more to the left, as well. As Aaron Boyd noted in his book, *First Lady: The Story of Hillary Rodham Clinton*, "Hillary's political beliefs changed from the conventional Republican ideas of her father, to the conventional Democratic ideas reflected in her friend Eldee Acheson."

Hillary continued to work with those less fortunate. She later told *Vanity Fair*, "All during my growing up years, I had a combined message of personal opportunity [and] public responsibility—that there were obligations that people who were as lucky as I was owed society."

One summer when she came home, Hillary went to Boston to attend a rally and protest parade in honor of the assassinated Martin Luther King, Jr. Hillary donned a black arm band and marched with the thousands of other protesters.

She also went to Chicago with her childhood friend, Betsy Johnson Ebeling, to see the demonstrations that turned into riots outside the Democratic National Convention. A police force of almost 12,000, along with 13,000 National Guardsmen and federal troops had been sent in to control peace protests that had gotten out of hand. In the end, over 1,000 demonstrators and over 190 policemen were injured, with about 100 demonstrators and 50 police hospitalized (an additional 63 people from the press were attacked by police). "We saw kids our age getting their heads beaten in. And the police were doing the beating," Ebeling says now. "Hillary and I just looked at each other. We had had a wonderful childhood in Park Ridge, but we obviously hadn't gotten the whole story."

A political science major set on law school, and a member of the student senate, Hillary found that her organizational skills were perfect for a '60s college activist. She protested curfews, fought to lift the ban on men in the dormitories, campaigned for greater minority student admission and crusaded for the extinction of mandatory classes.

During her senior year at Wellesley, Hillary served as president of the student government. She graduated with honors in 1969, and was the first graduating student ever at Wellesley to be allowed to speak at the commencement ceremony. This took quite a bit of maneuvering, but she was finally allowed by college president Ruth Adams to speak on the condition that her speech would not be embarrassing or reflect badly on the school. Adams would later regret this decision.

The guest speaker at commencement that year was Massachusetts Senator Edward

Brooke, a Republican who was also the first African-American Senator since the post-Civil War era. To the surprise of the audience and the team of students who helped prepare her speech, Hillary started out with some of her own comments criticizing Brooke for "being out of touch" with the times. Hillary's father, who had driven the long distance to see his shining star, later admitted to Martha Sherrill in her *Washington Post* story that he "wanted to lie on the ground and crawl away." Obviously not afraid to get her voice heard, even to the embarrassment of many others, Hillary had certainly taken her parents' teaching to heart. Shortly after her speech, *Life* magazine took up the story, featuring an earthy picture of her in hippie-style striped pants, balloon-sleeved shirt, sandals and no makeup.

At Wellesley, Hillary had definitely adopted the popular contempt for capitalism. A college boyfriend told David Maraniss, author of *First in His Class: A Biography of Bill Clinton*, that she had "grown up and out of the conservative materialistic mind-set which is typical of the suburbs. She was not interested in making money or being affluent." In her graduation speech, Hillary stated, "There are some things we feel—feelings that our prevailing acquisitive and competitive corporate life, including, tragically, universities, is not the way of life for us. We're searching for more immediate, ecstatic and penetrating modes of living." How easy it is to say these words, but as we shall see, how difficult it is to live by them!

After her commencement address,

Wellesley, Yale and Bill

Hillary practiced a little civil disobedience by swimming in Lake Waban, which was forbidden. She stripped down to her bathing suit, leaving behind her clothes and "Coke-bottle glasses," where they were confiscated by a guard. "Blind as a bat," she said, "I had to feel my way back to my room at Davis."

That summer, Hillary went to Alaska. There she traveled around and did odd jobs, including working in a fish cannery. She told the cannery owner that his fish looked a little black and weird and maybe not fit for consumption. He fired her.

Upon graduating from Wellesley, Hillary chose to attend Yale Law School, after deciding against Harvard, where a professor told her, "We don't need any more women." During her law school years, Hillary would continue her leftward shift, to the point of romanticizing Marxist ideals.

At Yale, Hillary continued her student activist lifestyle, protesting everything from the Vietnam war to the terribly unjust lack of Tampax machines in the women's restrooms. She also mediated meetings of students who had been tear-gassed during their demonstrations at the New Haven courthouse. Daniel Wattenberg, in an article titled "The Lady Macbeth of Little Rock," which appeared in the August 1992 edition of *The American Spectator*, wrote, "At Yale, Hillary slipped into an intellectual milieu marked by way-out and sometimes vicious left-wing polemics and activism." She struggled with the same ennui as the rest of the baby boom generation during the '60s.

ЈHE TOOK A VILLAGE

She spoke about it later, at Yale during the alumni weekend that coincided with the 1992 presidential campaign: "There was a great amount of ferment and confusion about what was and wasn't the proper role of law school education. We would have great arguments about whether we were selling out because we were getting a law degree, whether in fact we should be doing something else, not often defined clearly but certainly passionately argued. That we should somehow be 'out there,' wherever 'there' was, trying to help solve the problems that took up so much of our time in argument and discussion. Those were difficult and turbulent times, trying to reconcile the reasoned, ordered world we were studying with what we saw around us." Many of her classmates would go for the high-paying jobs and, eventually, so did Hillary. Apparently, the establishment is the enemy, unless it works in your favor.

For an example of just how far left Hillary had gone, one need only thumb through a few issues of the *Yale Review of Law and Social Action*, an "alternative" legal journal for which Hillary served on the editorial board. In *Boy Clinton*, R. Emmett Tyrrell, Jr. cites an article in the spring 1970 issue titled "Jamestown Seventy," written by James F. Blumstein and James Phelan. The article propounded "political migration to a single state for the purpose of gaining political control and establishing a living laboratory for experimentation." The authors elaborated on this by saying that "a new frontier must be found to foster further experimen-

20-3969

tation, an environment relatively unpolluted by conventional patterns of social and political organization. Experimentation with drugs, sex, individual lifestyles or radical rhetoric and action within the larger society is an insufficient alternative. Total experimentation is necessary. New ideas and values must be taken out of heads and transformed into reality."

Daniel Wattenberg, in his *American Spectator* article, mentioned that Hillary gave a "detailed sympathetic critique" of the article. In her view, Blumstein and Phelan were "long on rhetoric, short on action." As Tyrrell points out, "What 'action' Rodham had in mind has never been revealed."

Tyrrell also mentioned another issue of the *Review* where Hillary served as an associate editor. "That issue features cartoon drawings of policemen portrayed as pigs," he writes. "In one, a group of grotesque pigs is depicted marching with guns, slop dripping from gigantic snouts....In another cartoon a decapitated and dismembered pig is squealing in agony. The caption reads, 'Seize the Time!'" While Hillary was never arrested for any violent crimes, she associated with those who advocated it. Fortunately, views change, voting populations make demands, and husbands sign bills to put more police officers on the streets.

Hillary began to find her future path at Yale, deciding to focus on children's issues. Essential to her future path was Marian Wright Edelman, founder of the Washington Research Project and the Children's Defense Fund. Edelman was also a graduate of Yale Law

School, and was the first black woman to pass the bar in Mississippi. Hillary had read Edelman's article on civil rights in *Time* magazine, and eagerly attended a lecture Edelman gave at Yale. In Hillary's words, "In one of those strange twists of fate that enters all our lives if we're open to hear and to see them, I knew right away that I had to go to work for her."

With a small grant from Yale, Hillary interned for Edelman's research project in Washington, D.C. There, she went to work on Senator Walter Mondale's subcommittee doing an investigation into migrant labor camp conditions. Her passion for children's issues took root in her exploration into the sordid living conditions in which children of migrant laborers suffered.

Especially during Bill Clinton's various political campaigns, many people would take issue with the viewpoints that Edelman and Hillary upheld. According to Tyrrell, "In Edelman's case, behind the happy mask of the children's rights advocate, she and her acolytes steadily advance policies that undermine parents' control of their families, and shift power over children to the state. Edelman advertises herself as ensuring the rights of the young; actually she wants to increase the rights of the state over the young." Hillary's advocacy for children's rights turned toward taking away parental rights and control in a 1974 article, "Children Under the Law," which was reprinted in 1982 in the *Harvard Educational Review*. Tyrrell summarizes three measures for promoting children's rights that Hillary suggested in her article: "(1) the abolition of the legal category of minority and thus the reversal of a minor's presumption of legal incompetence; (2) extension to children of all procedural rights that are guaranteed to adults; and (3) an end to the legal presumption that there exists an identity of interests between children and their parents, thus allowing children to assert their own interests in the courts and opening the family to further judicial intrusion."

Years later, in 1979, Hillary told Martha Sherrill in an interview for the *Washington Post*: "Decisions about motherhood and abortion, schooling, cosmetic surgery, treatment of venereal disease, or employment, and others where the decision or lack of one will significantly affect the child's future should not be made unilaterally by parents. Children should have a right to be permitted to decide their own future if they are competent." This statement could only be made by someone who is not trying to raise a teenager!

In his *American Spectator* article, Daniel Wattenberg quoted Hillary: "The basic rationale for depriving people of rights in a dependency relationship is that certain individuals are incapable or undeserving of the right to take care of themselves and consequently need social institutions specifically designed to safeguard their position. Along with the family, past and present examples of such arrangements include marriage, slavery and the Indian reservation system." It seems that it would be difficult to keep children's rights in mind for one who slams marriage, comparing the family with slavery.

During the following summer, she worked for a public interest law firm. There is good reason to believe that Hillary became even more radical than her radical friends during this period. According to Tyrrell, Hillary "accepted the recommendations of two radical law professors and went to Oakland, California...to clerk in the law office of Robert Treuhaft, the communist husband of Jessica Mitford, known in her native United Kingdom as the 'Red Mitford' perhaps to distinguish her from her sister Unity Mitford who became infatuated with Hitler." Treuhaft took cases for the Black Panthers, Vietnam Veterans Against the War and other leftist causes. Hillary found herself caught up in the famous Black Panther murder trial, where leaders Bobby Seale and Erica Huggins were charged with murdering a Black Panther dissident. There were rumors that Hillary went to Sacramento with the Black Panthers when they disrupted the Legislature. Tyrrell continues, "To get a sense of precisely how stringent Rodham's politics had become by this time, it might be helpful to note that Treuhaft had joined the Communist party *after* the Hitler-Stalin Pact. He and his wife were *Stalinists*. Even the most doctrinaire sort of 1960s radicals gave Stalinists a wide berth. For a radical of a milder strength, such as a Coat and Tie Radical, associating with Stalinists was almost unimaginable.

Despite the progressive stance of her college years, however, Hillary began to face the realities of life. In his book, *Blood Sport: The President and His Adversaries*, James B. Stewart noted that "many of Hillary's Yale classmates who expressed similar rhetoric nonetheless easily made the transition to highly paid jobs at law firms, discovering that money not only provided a more comfortable existence, but could help realize their social and political ambitions." Hillary stuck to her guns for a short while, until she got her high-paying position at the Rose Law Firm in Arkansas, but as Stewart remarked, "Even at Yale, Hillary would buttonhole John Danner [a mutual friend of the Clinton's] for conversations about making money."

As for Hillary's social life, she had many friends with whom she liked to discuss intellectual matters. She dated a few Harvard and MIT students, but not seriously, and tended to prefer going out in groups. But it was at Yale that Hillary met Bill Clinton, who had been studying in England as a Rhodes Scholar. Bill's moderating influence would encourage Hillary's political pendulum to swing more to the right.

Their meeting has taken on legendary proportions in the media. Hillary first heard Bill in the Yale Student Union, asserting, "And not only that, but we grow the biggest watermelons in the world!"

Hillary asked her companion, "Who is that?"

Her companion replied, "Oh, that's Bill Clinton. He's from Arkansas, and that's all he ever talks about."

Later on, she was studying in the Yale Law School library, when she caught him staring at her and then looking away several times. Finally, she went up to him and said, "Look, if you're going to keep staring at me, then I'm going to keep looking back. And I think we ought to know each other's names. I'm Hillary Rodham."

Later, Bill would admit (probably the only time in his life), "I was dumbstruck. I couldn't think of my name."

In her book, *On the Make*, Meredith L. Oakley describes their early relationship. "Robert Reich, a fellow Rhodes Scholar, takes credit for urging them toward their first date. Their initial wariness was understandable. Bill was quite a man about town: dashing, extroverted, charming, and bright, but less devoted to his studies than most because of his consuming interest in politics and his amazing ability to memorize many facts and figures quickly and to store them for use at will. His class attendance was sporadic. Hillary was congenial and well liked but not exactly the comely type usually seen at Clinton's side. She was very serious about her studies and very involved in social issues. She required less company than Clinton, who seemingly has never met a stranger in his life. Constant fellowship and playing the field simply were not her style."

There are many stories about how the Clinton's shared a strong, mutual love and respect. In a May 14, 1993 article in the *Chicago Tribune*, Harlton Dalton (a Yale associate of the Clinton's) said, "Hillary is not easily charmed.

Wellesley, Yale and Bill

I don't believe she was charmed by Bill. She saw past the surface charm and [saw] someone who deeply wanted to make a difference and cared about the less fortunate."

According to ex-boyfriend Jeff Shields, as related in Judith Warner's biography *Hillary Clinton: The Inside Story*, Hillary had a "real interest in government from the point of view of someone who wanted to be involved and have an impact, but didn't know exactly how. She didn't have fixed ambitions in terms of knowing that she wanted to be elected to some office, and she certainly didn't give any indication that she was looking to attach herself to a politician—and I'm sure probably would have been offended by that concept if someone had raised it at that time."

It's hard to believe, however, that Hillary didn't know what she was getting into. She could certainly spot a diamond in the rough. In *The Unique Voice of Hillary Rodham Clinton*, a friend remembers Hillary remarking, "You know, Bill Clinton is going to be president of the United States someday!"

Even without great wealth to start with, their union has all the trappings of a marriage of convenience. Bill could take advantage of Hillary's assets as a strong-willed, forceful woman. Hillary knew long before she married him that he was not a one-woman kind of guy, but she could see that Bill would go far, enabling her to carry out her own agenda. For whatever reasons, within a year they were sharing a rented house in New Haven.

Hillary was scheduled to graduate a year

before Bill, but she chose to stay while he finished law school, under the auspices of studying child development at the Yale Child Study Center. Perhaps she really was furthering her career. Or maybe she was beginning to see through the eyes of those girls in high school she couldn't understand—the ones who put their lives aside for their boyfriends.

Bill's childhood was somewhat different than Hillary's. He was born on August 19, 1946 to Virginia Blythe. His father, William Jefferson Blythe III, had died in a car accident four months earlier. Bill lived with his grandparents in Hope, Arkansas while his mother studied nursing in New Orleans. She returned when he was four, and married Roger Clinton, a car dealer. Roger adopted Bill, whose name subsequently changed to William Jefferson Clinton. After they moved to Hot Springs, Arkansas, Bill's half-brother, Roger Clinton, Jr., was born.

Even at a young age, Bill found himself immersed in difficulties and controversy. While he was able to cover up his difficult childhood with the Arkansas press during his terms as governor, the national media managed to drag the story out of him and his mother during his presidential campaigning. Bill's stepfather, Roger Clinton, had been an abusive alcoholic, and Bill found himself constantly trying to either keep the peace or protect his mother. When Bill was four or five, his father, in a drunken rage, actually fired a .45-caliber revolver in the house, leaving a bullet hole in the wall.

As he got physically bigger, Bill began standing up to his stepfather. When he was 14, he broke down the door of his parents' bedroom while his father was abusing his mother. He said he was bigger than his father now, and there would be no more abuse. Later, he testified in court against his father to obtain an interlocutory decree of divorce between his parents.

For some unexplained reason, his mother remarried his stepfather shortly after their divorce become final in 1962. While Bill went on to excel in school and politics, his half-brother, Roger Clinton, Jr. ended up serving a year in prison for dealing cocaine.

In school, Bill was very popular and outgoing. He was active in student government and played tenor sax in the band. He graduated at the top of his class, winning a scholarship to Georgetown University in Washington, D.C. The years spent surviving his stepfather's drunken episodes no doubt had a profound effect on him, teaching him the skills necessary to survive the wide world of politics he was about to enter.

Everyone remembers hearing something about Bill's draft-dodging days that were exposed during his campaign for president. But how many know that he served in the Reserve Officers Training Corps during college? It's true. As a ROTC participant, Bill could not be called up for the draft. The downside was that if he decided to go for advanced ROTC training during his last two years of college, he would have to fulfill a two-year obligation of active duty after graduation. He didn't sign up for advanced ROTC training. He managed to avoid both active duty and the draft. With a little help from his friends.

In his book, *Clinton Confidential: The Climb to Power*, George Carpozi, Jr. outlines exactly how Clinton, who had reached 1-A draft status upon graduation, managed to evade the draft. He writes, "A multitude of strings were pulled from high places to give him a succession of delays that amounted to nearly 11 months over other draftees, who were allowed but a week to 10 days to answer their summonses to active duty."

Carpozi goes on to show how Bill's uncle, Raymond Clinton, submitted an application for Bill to enter the Naval Reserve. While there were no openings, this move gave him enough time to get his influential friends to urge the draft board to delay Bill's induction so he could go to Oxford as a Rhodes scholar (draft law did not provide deferments for postgraduate studies, except to medical school students).

While Bill denied he knew about any such attempts (his favorite tactic during all of the investigations into his dubious affairs), others had another story. In an interview with reporter Bill Rempel of the *Los Angeles Times*, Raymond Clinton's attorney, who helped in the campaign to prevent Bill's induction, said "Of course, Bill knew about it."

Bill's uncle pulled many strings from officials on high to get Bill into the Naval Reserve. Bill got in, but never showed up for his physical. His uncle had pulled even more strings to get his call-up delayed long enough for him to attend Oxford. In addition, Senator Fulbright, for whom Bill had interned on the Foreign Relations Committee, gave the draft board a little extra nudge. As the *Los Angeles Times* noted, "Bill Clinton was the only man of his prime draft age classified 1-A by the board in 1968 whose pre-induction physical examination was put off for 10½ months—more than twice as long as anyone else and more than five times longer than most area men of comparable eligibility."

After he returned home from Oxford, however, Bill found a draft induction notice waiting for him. Suddenly, his draft-dodging turned into the more serious induction avoidance. Senator Fulbright, again championing Bill's cause, helped get Bill back into the ROTC to evade the draft when there were no openings. Bill reneged on his commitment to serve in the ROTC.

When all was said and done, Bill managed to evade the draft and any commitment he made in his attempts to avoid induction as a private into the army.

After attending Oxford (where, he admitted in an MTV interview, he experimented with marijuana but "didn't inhale"), Bill accepted a scholarship to study law at Yale.

In 1972, Hillary and Bill campaigned for Democrat George McGovern, who lost by a landslide to Richard Nixon. During the campaign, Hillary became fast friends with Betsey Wright, who later worked for Bill when he was the governor of Arkansas.

In 1973, the couple went their separate ways for awhile, he to go back to Arkansas, she to work in Cambridge, Massachusetts for the Children's Defense Fund. In January of 1974, Hillary left for Washington, D.C. to work with the House Judiciary Committee in investigating Nixon's involvement in Watergate. She spent many hours transcribing the famous White House tapes and helping to prepare the impeachment proceedings against Nixon (perhaps a good training ground for learning trail-covering techniques). Here, she also became friends with Bernard Nussbaum, who served as the Clintons' first White House Counsel twenty years later, one of the first to fall in the style of Nixon in an ironic twist of fate.

Wellesley, Yale and Bill

Notes on Chapter 2

Page 15. *Vanity Fair*. May 1992.

Page 16. Boyd, Aaron. *First Lady: The Story of Hillary Rodham Clinton,* Greensboro: Morgan Reynolds, 1994.

Page 16. *Vanity Fair.*

Page 17. Sherrill, Martha. "Growing Up Hillary," Part two of three, *Washington Post,* January 20, 1993.

Page 18. Sherrill, Martha. "Growing Up Hillary."

Page 18. Marannis, David. *First in His Class: A Biography of Bill Clinton,* New York: Simon & Schuster, 1995.

Page 19. Sherrill, Martha. "Growing Up Hillary."

Page 19. Wattenberg, Daniel. "The Lady Macbeth of Little Rock," *The American Spector,* August 1992.

Page 20. Tyrrell, R. Emmett, Jr. *Boy Clinton: The Political Biography,* Washington, D.C.: Regnery Publishing, Inc., 1996.

Page 21. Wattenberg, Daniel. "The Lady Macbeth of Little Rock."

Page 21. Tyrrell, R. Emmett, Jr. *Boy Clinton.*

Page 22. Tyrrell, R. Emmett, Jr. *Boy Clinton.*

Page 22. Rodham, Hillary. "Children Under the Law," *Harvard Educational Review,* 1982.

Page 23. Sherrill, Martha. *Washington Post,* 1979.

Page 23. Wattenberg, Daniel. "The Lady Macbeth of Little Rock."

Page 24. Tyrrell, R. Emmett, Jr. *Boy Clinton.*

Page 25. Stewart, James B. *Blood Sport: The President and His Adversaries,* New York: Simon & Schuster, 1996.

Page 26. Oakley, Meredith L. *On the Make: The Rise of Bill Clinton*, Washington, D.C.: Regnery Publishing, 1994.

Page 26. Dalton, Harlton. *Chicago Tribune*, May 14, 1993.

Page 27. Warner, Judith. *Hillary Clinton: The Inside Story*.

Page 27. Osborne, Claire G., ed. *The Unique Voice of Hillary Rodham Clinton: A Portrait in Her Own Words*, New York: Avon Books, 1997.

Page 30. Carpozi, George, Jr. *Clinton Confidential: The Climb to Power*.

Page 30. Rempel, Bill. *Los Angeles Times*.

Page 31. *Los Angeles Times*.

Page 31. *MTV*.

3

Arkansas

First the "Bear State," then the "Wonder State." Finally, a legislature with a taste for the ironic decided to package Arkansas as "The Land of Opportunity." When the Clintons set their sights on this state, it was the second poorest in the U.S., behind only Mississippi. True, Arkansas is rich in natural resources, including timber, petroleum, minerals and natural gas, but that makes the "opportunity" for the wheelers and dealers: business tycoons and politicians. And, of course, lawyers.

The elite class formed only a small percentage of Arkansas's total population, however. In his article, "The Name of Rose," which appeared in the April 4, 1994 edition of *New Republic*, L. J. Davis describes the squalor the rest of the state lived in: "It bears a close resemblance to a Third World country, with a ruling oligarchy, a small and relatively powerless middle class, and a disfranchised, leaderless populace admired for its colorful folkways, deplored for its propensity to violence (on a per capita basis, Little Rock has one of the highest murder rates in the nation), and appreciated for its willingness to do just about any kind of work for just about any kind of wage." We'll see later how the Clintons were mysteriously surrounded by more than their fair share of "murder rates" and puzzling acts of violence.

Unions that the rest of the nation might consider odd were commonplace in Arkansas. In his January 24, 1994 *Newsweek* article, "Big Times in Little Rock," Howard Fineman reports on this marriage of the private sector and government: "Many fortunes were built on politically influenced deals at the intersection of private markets and government: regulated utilities, municipal bonds, state banks....Out of the way, with a small population—and essentially controlled by one party, the Democrats, since the Civil War—Arkansas produced an elite that generally dealt only with itself and that viewed conflicts of interest as business as usual."

All obvious and tasteless jokes about close family ties in Arkansas aside, the interrelationships between business and politics are often dizzyingly circular. In his monograph, *Boy Clinton*, R. Emmett Tyrrell, Jr. cites a few examples. He writes, "In Arkansas it is not considered unseemly for the owner of Anthony Forest Products, Beryl Anthony, Sr., to be chairing the state forestry commission; and so much the better that Beryl Anthony, Jr., has served in the United States Congress and that his wife was the sister of an influential partner at the Rose Law Firm—Vince Foster, now deceased. The Arkansas Poultry Federation recently had on its payroll the chairman of the state's Senate agriculture committee. In fact, lobbyists for the state's chicken producers are regularly members of the state legislature."

Bill Clinton took full advantage of this brotherhood. Tyrrell continues, "Don Tyson, chairman of Tyson Foods, Inc. (and architect of the Rock Cornish hen), has bragged publicly that he contributed to Bill Clinton's first gubernatorial campaign in 1978 in return for Clinton's promise to raise the ceiling on the weight that a poultry truck may bear in lugging its feathered products over state roads. Tyson is equally boastful of how he shifted his campaign contributions from Clinton to his 1980 Repulican challenger after Clinton failed to make good on that promise. Arguably, Clinton's failure to return Tyson's favor cost him the 1980 election. Arguably, too, the favor was a bribe, at least as the term is understood in jurisdictions beyond Arkansas."

Into this brave, new world of politics that may be termed amoral, at best, stepped the Clintons. While they may have had a fairly modest beginning in Arkansas, they quickly gathered momentum and took the state by storm.

Although Hillary's work and her demeanor impressed many prestigious Washington law firms, and she received several offers, she followed her man to Fayetteville, where Bill taught at the University of Arkansas.

Sara Ehrman, Hillary's roommate and friend in Washington, D.C., drove with Hillary to Arkansas. In an interview with Martha Sherrill for the *Washington Post*, she said, "I told her every twenty minutes that she was crazy to bury herself in Fayetteville," says Ehrman. "'You are crazy. You are out of your mind. You're going to this rural, remote place—and wind up married to some country lawyer." But Hillary went because she "had to" and because she loved him. And, of course, she knew that Bill was the key to power.

Hillary's friend, Carolyn Ellis, pointed out in Judith Warner's biography, *Hillary Clinton: The Inside Story*, 'She wanted to have her own independent life. She knew that he was going to do things political and go into public service, run for office. I think there was some fear on her part that she would simply be an adjunct to him. That was the traditional thing that we had seen up until that point. My response at that time was that she had no political base of her own, and she could do an awful lot down in Arkansas with her talent. I guess the only thing that surprised me is that it took her so long to go to Arkansas.

"Eventually she made an emotional decision. And she seemed so much more certain of herself once she went."

While her friends may romanticize her move, it is worth considering which emotions this decision was based upon. Hillary was al-

ready known by those close to her as having a
stormy temper, and everyone, including
Hillary, knew full well about Bill's arrogant
sexual escapades. There are several reports of
the Clintons' near breakups, but Bill put up
with Hillary's humors, and she turned a blind
eye to his shenanigans. For both, this was to
be a marriage of convenience.

Hillary's temper indeed took on legendary proportions, and arguments between the
two Clintons erupted frequently. In her article,
"Hillary the Pol," in the May 30, 1994 edition
of the *New Yorker*, Connie Bruck describes her
devastating disposition, "Temper is a trait she
and Bill Clinton share, but, while his is said to
erupt with the force of a sudden squall and then
be spent—leaving him, more often than not,
eager to make amends—hers has inspired on-
going fear in some of those who have worked
with her over the years. Grown men describe
her as being, at such times, scary." Her out-
bursts, not by any means contained to her husband, helped to earn her such nicknames as
"Hillary the Hun," "The Iron Lady of Little
Rock," "The Lady Macbeth of Little Rock,"
"Yippie Wife From Hell," "The Dragon Lady"
and other colorful epithets.

But in their early years in Fayetteville,
where Hillary took a job at the University of
Arkansas law school teaching criminal law, civil
procedure and children's law, she earned a
much milder nickname, and became known in
the small town as "The Lady Lawyer." She was
known for being an intimidating taskmaster,
aggressive, blunt and very articulate.

SHE TOOK A VILLAGE

Not satisfied with performing only one activity at a time, Hillary set up a legal aid clinic and a program to promote student involvement with prison inmates. With all of her accomplishments, her name began to appear in the paper and TV newscasts more frequently than her husband's. She commanded wide media attention with her efforts to pass a law through the state legislature requiring judges rule from the bench whether evidence of a rape victim's prior sexual behavior was admissible before being presented to a jury. While this bill didn't make it out of committee, she successfully campaigned for the establishment of the first rape crisis center in Fayetteville, and she instituted a program of education for women on sexual violence. One has to wonder if this was a response to the arrogant way Bill Clinton repeatedly treated the women in his life.

During this time, Hillary took over Bill's first political campaign to unseat Republican Representative John Paul Hammerschmidt. She organized the campaign, delegating tasks, arranging Bill's schedule and writing his speeches. She even brought her Republican family to Arkansas to help. Bill may have had the charisma, but as Aaron Boyd noted in his biography of Hillary, he told reporters that Hillary was "far better organized, more in control, more intelligent and more eloquent than I am." Bill lost the race with 48.2% of the vote, a close call for an incumbent running against a virtual nobody.

Hillary and Bill were married on October 11, 1975. In her own words, as quoted in

Arkansas

The Unique Voice of Hillary Rodham Clinton, Bill "was a defeated politician when I married him." She set him straight, however. Even at their wedding, it became clear what their intentions were for this relationship. As George Carpozi, Jr. relates in *Clinton Confidential: The Climb to Power*, at their wedding reception, Bill announced, as if repeating his marriage vows, "We are gathered here today to witness the joining of two people...who'll be deeply involved in the political wars of 1976." He had decided that, instead of making another run against Hammerschmidt for a congressional seat, he would run for state Attorney General, after learning Attorney General Jim Guy Tucker was aiming for a higher office.

The wedding itself was fairly unremarkable, and the reasons for it were basically political. As Meredith Oakley points out in *On the Make*, "Marriage wasn't a requirement for Arkansas politicians, but it was recommended, and however liberal Fayetteville might seem, the two felt they could not live together publicly without being married." Oakley goes on to say that the wedding "was a hastily assembled affair. Hillary bought her wedding gown, a Victorian-style linen dress trimmed in lace, 'off the rack' at a local department store the night before. A small ceremony before their immediate families was followed by a larger one before almost three hundred friends and colleagues from Boston, New Haven, Washington, and Fayetteville." At their union, Hillary dropped a bombshell that she would later regret: she would definitely keep her maiden name.

Their honeymoon was a family affair. Hillary's parents and brothers went with the newlyweds to Acapulco. Upon their return, Clinton put in his bid to run for Attorney General. Stephen A. Smith, campaign manager for the 1976 campaign, described it in *The Clintons of Arkansas*: "announced in March and over in May, he won a clear majority in the primary against two opponents and faced no Republican opposition in the general election." This wasn't just a fluke, however; Bill had been industriously expanding his contacts among the Arkansas elite since he had narrowly lost his run for congress. Ironically, Bill's campaign slogan was "Character, Competence, and Concern." There are more than a few women out there who would agree he's a character, all right!

Apart from a few raised eyebrows about the use of her maiden name, and a few snickers about who was bringing home the real bacon when Bill said they could subsist on the $6,000 annual salary of an attorney general, Hillary played only a behind-the-scenes role in the campaign for Attorney General.

When Bill was elected as the Arkansas Attorney General in 1976, the Clintons moved to the state capital in Little Rock. At this time, Hillary accepted an offer with the Rose Law Firm, where she became known for her analytical mind and brusque manner, and where she made some of the contacts whose names we still see splashed in the media time and again.

During Bill's 1978 campaign for governor of Arkansas, Hillary continued to be his chief advisor, but received a lot of criticism for keeping her maiden name and having a career outside the home. Nevertheless, in 1979 at the tender age of thirty-two, Bill became the youngest governor in the United States.

Criticism of Hillary continued throughout Bill's term as governor, mostly about her hair, her attire and her feminist attitude. Critics were harsh. Tyrrell describes her in their first term in the Governor's Mansion: "She arrived at the mansion overweight, wore her hair long and unkempt, and went without make-up or perfumes. Her spectacles were as thick as bullet-proof glass, and the lenses were encased in impressively ugly frames. The dresses that she wore were frumpy, though she often wore pants, usually baggy corduroys or jeans." She had not yet mastered the public relations aspect of being the first lady, and was even caught in a photo reading a book while Bill and everyone around her cheered and waved.

When their daughter Chelsea (named after Judy Collins's song, "Chelsea Morning") was born on February 27, 1980, a newspaper announcement read, "Governor Bill Clinton and Hillary Rodham have a daughter." This implication that they were not married did not help Clinton in his 1980 campaign. Hillary stood fast on her feminist ways for as long as she could, but with her refusal to be the perfect wife and his to be the perfect political pawn, Bill earned another dubious distinction in 1980 by becoming the youngest ex-governor in the United States.

JHE TOOK A VILLAGE

While waiting for the 1982 race for governor, Bill took a position with Wright, Lindsey and Jennings, a competitor of the Rose Law Firm. After Chelsea's birth, Hillary returned full time to the Rose Law Firm, where she earned over $100,000 a year, a tad more than her husband's $35,000 salary. During this time, Bill learned to keep his constituents happy (at least, the ones that mattered with their wealth and power), and Hillary, too, bowed to the pressure of the establishment. She lost weight and got a new 'do, new glasses and new wardrobe. She also took her husband's name, and attended his Southern Baptist church, even though it was at her insistence that they be married by a Methodist minister.

Thus it was, as with many others of their generation, that their "karma ran over their dogma" and they both became well established on the road to bending their beliefs when and where it suited them best.

It paid off. Although she had softened her image for the 1982 campaign, Hillary put all her strength into the campaign trail. Her friends, Betsey Wright and Susan McDougal joined the Clintons in their run for the governorship. In his tell-all book, *Blood Sport: The President and His Adversaries*, James B. Stewart recounts the following story showing how Hillary may not have been completely transformed into the perfect wife. He writes that "the new facade didn't entirely suppress Hillary's nature. Much like Bill, Susan loved campaigning—all the hugging and glad-handing and getting to know people from all over

44

the state. Hillary, by contrast, usually looked slightly pained by the experience. On one occasion when the McDougals and Clintons appeared together, a woman came rushing up to Hillary. 'I made these for you, honey,' she said. 'I just think so much of your husband.' Beaming, she handed Hillary a pair of earrings in the shape of hogs—the Arkansas Razorback mascot. Susan thought they were so cute she would have put them on then and there and worn them for weeks. Hillary mustered a thank-you, then the woman asked her to put them on. Hillary wouldn't. With the woman out of earshot, she turned to Susan. 'This is the kind of shit I have to put up with.'"

Nonetheless, she and her friends managed Bill's campaign with efficiency and toughness. Bill won with 54.7% of the vote, a comeback he owed largely to Hillary and, of course, his mollified business and political cronies. In his own words, taken by Meredith Oakley for the June 28, 1983 edition of the *Arkansas Democrat*, "I think I have to do a better job than I did when I was here before in keeping in touch with my friends and supporters, who put me here."

One of the major items on Bill's agenda was education reform for Arkansas, which ranked very poorly in national education surveys. He formed an information-gathering committee to assess the state's educational system, and selected Hillary as the chair. As quoted in Aaron Boyd's biography, *First Lady: The Story of Hillary Rodham Clinton*, Bill announced that this would "guarantee that I will have a person who is closer to me than anyone

else, overseeing a project that is more important than anything else. I don't know if it's a
politically wise move, but it's the right thing to
do."

The "Hillary Committee," as it was soon
to become known, toured the state and came
up with a list of recommendations, including
such well-supported ones as mandatory kinder-
garten and smaller class sizes. The reform bill
also advocated teacher competency testing,
which sparked a controversy that gained national attention. Despite boos and catcalls from
teachers when she toured schools, Hillary lob-
bied hard for the legislature to pass the bill. As
Boyd relates, one politician quipped, "It looks
like we've elected the wrong Clinton." Hillary
saw her efforts pay off in 1985, when most of
the reforms became law.

Another of Hillary's accomplishments
during their term as governor was instituting a
program called Home Instruction Program for
Preschool Youngsters, or HIPPY. This successful program continues to this day in Arkansas.
Its purpose is to bring teachers into the homes
of disadvantaged preschoolers to teach parents
how to help their children prepare for school.
Studies showed that these children fared much
better in school than those who received no preschool instruction. Hillary gained a national
reputation for child advocacy.

At the same time she made these great
accomplishments, however, Hillary was still
perfecting the other of her two faces. Torn between her desire to do good and her desire to
acquire wealth and power, she managed to do

both during Bill's second term as governor.

Hillary continued with the Rose Law Firm, specializing in copyright law. She worked hard, often staying in the office until midnight. Within two years of joining, Hillary became a partner of the firm by a unanimous vote, the first woman partner in the firm's history.

It was fortunate for her that they lived in Arkansas, where the obvious is politely ignored. Conflicts of interest abounded in her practice and in her extracurricular positions on the boards of several powerful companies. As Meredith Oakley points out in *On the Make*, Hillary's business with the Rose Law Firm "occasionally took her before state regulatory agencies whose administrators and regulatory boards had been appointed by her husband, but as the spouse of a constitutional officer, she was not required by state ethics laws to disclose any potential conflicts of interest."

In the 1980s, Hillary served as a paid director on several corporate boards, including TCBY yogurt company, La Farge (a French chemical company), WalMart and Tyson Foods. Her relationship with Tyson Foods raised a few eyebrows during the governorship and years later during the Whitewater investigations. Many thought it a conflict of interest that the governor's wife should be on the board of a company that was clearly responsible for polluting some of the rivers and streams in Arkansas, although no charges were brought stating that actual laws were broken.

Notes on Chapter 3

Page 35. Davis, L.J. "The Name of Rose," *New Republic*, April 4, 1994.

Page 36. Fineman, Howard. "Big Times in Little Rock," *Newsweek*, January 24, 1994.

Page 36. Tyrrell, R. Emmett, Jr. *Boy Clinton: The Political Biography*, Washington, D.C.: Regnery Publishing, Inc., 1996.

Page 37. Tyrrell, R. Emmett, Jr. *Boy Clinton*.

Page 38. Sherrill, Martha. "The Retooling of the Political Wife," *Washington Post*, January 13, 1993.

Page 38. Warner, Judith. *Hillary Clinton: The Inside Story*.

Page 39. Bruck, Connie. "Hillary the Pol," *The New Yorker*, May 30, 1994.

Page 40. Boyd, Aaron. *First Lady: The Story of Hillary Rodham Clinton*, Greensboro: Morgan Reynolds, 1994.

Page 41. Osborne, Claire G., ed. *The Unique Voice of Hillary Rodham Clinton: A Portrait in Her Own Words*, New York: Avon Books, 1997.

Page 41. Carpozi, George, Jr. *Clinton Confidential: The Climb to Power*.

Page 41. Oakley, Meredith L. *On the Make: The Rise of Bill Clinton*, Washington, D.C.: Regnery Publishing, 1994.

Page 42. Dumas, Ernest, ed. *The Clintons of Arkansas: An Introduction by Those Who Know Them Best*, Fayetteville, Arkansas: University of Arkansas Press, 1993.

Page 43. Tyrrell, R. Emmett, Jr. *Boy Clinton*.

Page 44. Stewart, James B. *Blood Sport: The President and His Adversaries*, New York: Simon & Schuster, 1996.

Arkansas

Page 45. Oakley, Meredith. *Arkansas Democrat*, June 28, 1998.

Page 45. Boyd, Aaron. *First Lady*.

Page 46. Boyd, Aaron. *First Lady*.

Page 47. Oakley, Meredith L. *On the Make*.

4
Eyes on the Presidency

After winning back the governorship in 1982, Bill was reelected in 1984 and 1986. This last run was for a four-year term. With his mind on loftier ideas, Bill continued his ardent networking, expanding to a national level. He became chairman of the National Governors Association in 1986. Clinton's plans to run for president were so set that he rented a ballroom at the Excelsior Hotel in Little Rock to announce his intentions. In a baffling move for a young governor with such strong potential to win the Democratic ticket, Clinton cancelled the shindig and issued a press statement.

Bill's stated reason for not running for President in 1988 was because Chelsea was only seven, and the long periods of separation would be too hard on her. In an interview recounted in *The Unique Voice of Hillary Rodham Clinton*, Hillary agreed, "Looking back on it, he was right. That wasn't the time."

It wasn't the time for Bill to run for President. It *was*, however, the time for media attacks on candidates' "indiscretions." It was the Year of the Sex Scandal. Everyone remembers how the media gleefully took Gary Hart up on his invitation to follow him—right into the arms of Donna Rice.

In his bestseller book, *The Agenda*, Bob Woodward of Watergate fame writes, "Clinton had spoken to friends about the issue before. He had confided to another friend over dinner one night four years earlier the nature of his dilemma. It was the late summer of 1987 and Clinton had just decided not to run for president in the 1988 campaign. You know why I'm not running for president? Clinton asked. The friend guessed that infidelity was the reason....Clinton acknowledged he had strayed." Shrewdly, Clinton guessed that the adultery issue was only a passing fad for that election year.

It wasn't a big secret that Bill had "strayed." And often. In a scandal that would become known as Troopergate, the media discovered that Bill had been arrogantly using Arkansas state troopers at taxpayer expense to ferry him back and forth to his paramour, Gennifer Flowers. Roger Perry, Larry Patterson and Danny Ferguson were the most well-known of the troopers, constituting the old guard, which had stayed on from governor to governor. In Arkansas, state troopers are assigned to be the governor's bodyguard, chauffeur and general personal assistant. They began to suspect something when certain calls they tried to patch through to Bill while Hillary was around were met with "take a message," while the same calls would go right through when Hillary was gone.

The troopers would often find themselves chauffeuring Clinton to the same place, sometimes waiting for hours for him to return to the car. In *Blood Sport: The President and His Adversaries*, James B. Stewart writes, "Patterson often drove Clinton to Quapaw Towers, the apartment complex where Flowers lived. Clinton told him that he had to go there for meetings with Maurice Smith, the former aide who also had an apartment there. Patterson would wait in the car while Clinton was inside, often for extended periods. He doubted that Clinton was making such frequent visits to discuss political strategy. Smith was a notorious cigar smoker, yet Clinton often returned smelling of perfume."

There is no doubt that Hillary knew what her husband was doing. Perry remembers an incident when he had lent Bill his car so Bill could go off galavanting without being recognized. Hillary found out he was gone, and had a good idea of what he was up to. Perry called Clinton on a cellular phone to let him know. Stewart relates, "About fifteen minutes later, Perry's car came screeching up to the mansion's kitchen door. Bill jumped out, leaving the door open. When Perry went to close it and retrieve his car, he could hear Hillary and Bill arguing in the kitchen. They were shouting. Perry left, trying not to overhear, uncomfortable about intruding on their privacy. About two hours later, he went into the kitchen. A cupboard door was broken off its hinges. Food, pots and pans, broken glass were scattered on the floor. Perry cleaned up the glass. Prison inmates working on the grounds and in maintenance cleaned up the rest."

Let's face it—Hillary got the short end of the stick when it comes to fidelity issues. She has admirably handled all the bad press her husband received with his many mistresses. It leaves us all wondering why such a strong-willed, attractive and bright woman would tolerate—even publicly support—so many extra-marital affairs. But then again, one never knows what goes on behind other peoples' closed bedroom doors.

Hillary did a lot of damage control in the media regarding her husband's infidelities. Various close acquaintances have reported raging battles in the Clintons' relatively private living quarters. But Hillary did what she said wasn't in her character, took the advice of the Tammy Wynette song she would later publicly denounce, and stood by her man. Adoringly.

Why would she do that? While she may make public assertions about how much she loves her husband, there must be something even stronger than love that binds them together: power.

While Hillary has denied that they worked out some kind of "open marriage," those close to her have suggested otherwise. In

1985, there were reports that Hillary was ready to end the marriage. During the 1992 presidential campaign, Hillary replied in an interview with David Frost after he asked whether she had considered divorce during their troubled years, "Not seriously...no, no...I mean...I never doubted and I know he never did either, that not only do we love each other, but that we are committed to each other. That love was something so much a part of us that it was impossible to think of ending or cutting it off or moving beyond it."

During an interview with *Glamour*, she said, "Bill and I have always loved each other. No marriage is perfect, but just because it isn't perfect doesn't mean the only solution is to walk off and leave it. A marriage is always growing and changing. We couldn't say, 'Well, this isn't ideal' and get a divorce. I'm proud of my marriage. I have women friends who chose not to marry, or who married and chose not to have children, or who married and then divorced, or who had children on their own. That's okay, that's their choice. This is my choice. This is how I define my personhood—Bill and Chelsea."

During their troubled years (we might ask, which years weren't?), the Clintons saw a therapist. During that time, some saw Bill sink into periods of depression, with "a tendency to be self-destructive because he viewed himself as a failure." Despite his various realizations during therapy, there is quite a bit of evidence that he continued his adulterous lifestyle right through his tenure in the White House. Hillary apparently came out of the sessions with even more steel added to her resolve to stay in control of their marriage, the presidency and their future.

In *Clinton Confidential*, Carpozi writes, "Although Clinton didn't wish to discuss his infidelities with Hillary..., he was compelled to, over and over. She demanded that he do so. That is, until Hillary realized in psychotherapy—in sessions with a University of Arkansas psychiatrist—that her husband's marital unfaithfulness was an incurable weakness, indeed a disease. From that understanding evolved the 'open marriage' compact.... Through it all, Hillary appeared to be standing loyally by Bill, always shielding him from the stares of those who would exploit his vulnerability to other women."

In 1990, when Bill chose to run for governor yet again, even though it probably wasn't in Arkansas's best interests to have a governor distracted by designs on the presidency, he battled with Republican Larry Nichols. Nichols' campaign focused largely on Bill's moral character. Even after intensive marriage counseling, Bill couldn't keep the faith. Nichols managed to come up with a lengthy list of Bill's "asides." Among the prestigious names were: Sherry, owner of the Something Special Boutique; Beverly Lindsey, state coordinator of Mondale's 1984 campaign; Helen Van Berg; and Beth Coulson, an Appeals Court judge appointed by Clinton.

From this arose yet another scandal: a lawsuit by Robert McIntosh for $20,000 he said

Clinton owed him as "hush money." In *Clinton Confidential*, George Carpozi expands on the details of this lawsuit:

"McIntosh claimed he was hired by Clinton as a 'Mr. Fix-it' to derail Larry Nichols' efforts to expose the governor's secrets about favors he received from both the ADFA [Arkansas Development Finance Authority, where Nichols believed Bill was using a slush fund to finance his encounters] and his women.

"'I was promised twenty-five thousand dollars by Clinton to show up wherever Nichols was speaking and brand him a Republican mole,' fumed McIntosh. 'And I did a good job. But all he paid me was five-thousand dollars. He still owes me twenty thousand and won't put it up. That's why I'm suing him.'"

Hillary chose to put up with her husband's philandering. Bill wasn't always necessarily discreet with her, either. He invited Gennifer to sing at the governor's mansion for the celebration of the Clintons' eleventh anniversary. Events indicate Hillary knew full well exactly what Gennifer meant to her husband. Carpozi relates the following interview with Gennifer:

"'I knew she knew,' Gennifer Flowers would say in 1992, after her 12-year affair with Bill Clinton had run its course. 'Hillary avoided looking at me all night long. I felt peculiar being there, but I didn't want to disappoint Bill.'

"The highlight of the evening—more precisely described as a 'perilously close call'—occurred in a second-floor hallway where Bill had steered Gennifer for some out-of-bounds monkey business.

"'Come on, nobody's in there ... let's go in and get a quick one off,' Gennifer said Bill pleaded with her.

"They were standing outside the men's room.

"'You're crazy!' I almost screamed out. 'What if Hillary should catch us?'

"'Oh, you worry too much,' Gennifer quoted Clinton's protest. 'She'll never be the wiser.'

"'Just then, who should come sauntering along the hallway?' Gennifer asked.

"'It was Hillary. She passed us with her gaze straight ahead, walking like a zombie. She didn't acknowledge Bill, and she seemed to want to regard my presence even less.'"

Hillary may not have been happy with it, but she stuck it out. Bill obviously wasn't satisfied by Hillary's bedroom performance. They were a partnership; together, they were too powerful to let a few little affairs get in the way. The truth was, Bill needed her. And Hillary needed him.

Even though Bill escaped close national media scrutiny by electing not to run for the presidency just yet, he still managed to nearly ruin his political career at the 1988 Democratic National Convention, where he delivered a speech that contained lengthy additions provided by the Dukakis campaign staff. His fifteen-minute speech turned into thirty-three minutes. When he paused, the crowd yelled "We want Mike!" His protest to this treatment was met with boos and catcalls. He was visibly perspiring. ABC and NBC cut to other coverage of the convention, and John Chancellor commented, "I am afraid that one of the most attractive governors just put a blot on his record."

Clinton was applauded only when he said, "And now, in closing..." *The Washington Post* article on his speech was titled "The Numb and the Restless," and on *The Tonight Show*, Johnny Carson quipped, "The surgeon general has just approved Bill Clinton as an over-the-counter sleep aid. What a windbag!"

In a brilliant move to save his career, Hillary managed to convince Bill to appear on *The Tonight Show*. The producers had agreed to have him on the show if he played his saxophone with the band. Johnny Carson's rambling monologue was a brutal parody of the convention speech, but Clinton laughed at Carson's pokes. Carson admitted Clinton's good humor, and Clinton received favorable national media coverage for his ability to joke about himself.

Bill's political career was saved, and he had Hillary to thank for it.

They were to become a powerful team. When the time came to announce their bid for the 1992 presidency, they sold themselves as a package deal. Hillary was quoted in the *Unique Voice of Hillary Rodham Clinton* as saying, "If you vote for my husband, you get me; it's a two-for-one, blue-plate special."

Hillary basically ran the campaign, demanding it be headquartered in Little Rock instead of Washington, D.C., where his campaign staff wanted it. No doubt she felt safer in Arkansas, and could stifle rumors (true or not) quicker there.

In *Clinton Confidential*, Carpozi writes, "The Clinton campaign was to be masterminded by the one the newshawks had singled out as a candidate in the unofficial presidential sweepstakes—Hillary Clinton. As soon as the announcement was made, she began rounding up a bunch of hometown pals from Park Ridge to work in the campaign.

"'I don't trust those quacks Bill has as his advisers to get him off the ground in this do-or-die drive for the White House,' Hillary was overheard to say. 'I'm calling in my friends to jiggle the nerve centers that'll elect my Bill to the presidency.'

"Hillary's friends descended upon Little Rock, got their marching orders, and then spread out over the landscape.

"While people like James Carville, George Stephanopoulos, Dee Dee Myers, Betsey Wright, and other advisers carried the Clinton banner into the upcoming presidential primaries, Hillary Clinton led the charge.

"She had the first and last word about anything and everything that the candidate was to do. Bill Clinton was the puppet and the head puppeteer was Hillary Clinton."

First on the agenda: what to do about this woman thing?

A poll in *USA Today* sounded her call to action. The poll found that 39 percent of respondents would not vote for a candidate cheating on his wife without her knowledge, but that 65 percent would vote for him if he came clear with her. So Hillary urged her husband to speak candidly about their marriage. Shortly before announcing his candidacy, he spoke at a National Press Club breakfast, in front of the likes of Dan Rather, Larry King, Ted Koppel and other media bigwigs. "Like nearly anybody that's been together twenty years," he said, "our relationship has not been perfect or free of difficulties. But we feel good about where we are. We believe in our obligations and we intend to be together thirty or forty years from now, regardless of whether I run for president or not."

It was a shrewd move, and a well-timed one at that. The media had had its fill of womanizing politicians during the 1988 campaign. Respectable publications such as the *New York Times* developed a policy to leave affairs as tabloid fodder. If anything, his philandering gave him a "human" edge, and this charismatic governor from an obscure part of the country became a favorite contender for the media, who could see a good story if nothing else. With the Clintons' dealings, they struck the mother lode.

Strike one came when the *Star* hit the newsstands with Gennifer Flowers' bombshell, "My 12-Year Affair with Bill Clinton," backed up by "The Secret Love Tapes That Prove It!" Shortly after, Betsey Wright joined the campaign to counteract any further "bimbo eruptions." Ms. Wright had been a long-time acquaintance of Bill's since serving with him on the McGovern committee, and had been brought in to help orchestrate Bill's comeback after losing the Arkansas governorship. In *Blood Sport*, James B. Stewart describes her as devoted and tough. "Like Hillary," he writes, "she was the kind of woman who could argue with Bill, discipline him from time to time, keep him focused and on course. She also had an instinctive kinship with Hillary, and she was no romantic threat. Indeed, some people in the campaign assumed that one of her functions was to keep Bill's amorous impulses in check and to protect his political future." Betsey would keep very busy during the presidential campaign.

Hillary did her part to keep the bimbo factor muted, turning the media into an asset rather than a dragon she wanted to slay. She and the others running the campaign knew they had to tackle the issue head-on. Hillary rejected appearing on *Nightline* with Ted Koppel, knowing that her husband couldn't possibly withstand Koppel's cross-examination. Instead, she managed to arrange for a special fifteen-minute edition of *60 Minutes* to air after the Superbowl. Insiders say that *60 Minutes* interviewer Steve Kroft was given the questions to ask and was ordered not to stray from the list.

Hillary and Bill appeared on the segment together, with Bill giving squirrely answers to Kroft's questions. For example, Kroft said, "[Gennifer Flowers] is alleging and has described in some detail in a supermarket tabloid what she calls a twelve-year affair with you." Bill's response was, "*That* allegation is false." Kroft's follow-up consisted of: "I am assuming from your answer that you're categorically denying that you ever had an affair with Gennifer Flowers." Clinton got himself off the hook with: "I've said that before, and so has she."

Eyes on the Presidency

When Kroft asked Bill if he had had any extramarital affairs, Clinton replied, "I have acknowledged wrongdoing. I have acknowledged causing pain in my marriage. I have said things to you and to the American people from the beginning, that no American politician ever has. I think most Americans watching this tonight will know what we're saying. They'll get it and they'll feel that we have been more candid, and I think what the press has to decide is, are we going to engage in a game of 'gotcha'?"

Hillary won the public over when she told Kroft, "There isn't a person watching this who would feel comfortable sitting on this couch detailing everything that ever went on in their life or their marriage, and I think it's real dangerous in this country if we don't have a zone of privacy for everybody."

The interview was a stroke of genius. The Clintons managed to portray themselves as a devoted couple intent on strengthening their marriage. They managed to make Bill's womanizing into a problem the rest of the country could identify with. Hillary almost blew it with one comment, however.

She made the unfortunate remark that "I'm not sitting here because I'm some little woman standing by my man, like Tammy Wynette. I'm sitting here because I love him and I respect him and I honor what he's been through and what we've been through together, and you know, if that's not enough for the people, then heck, don't vote for him."

In *Clinton Confidential*, George Carpozi, Jr. relates that Miss Wynette (whose hit song

"Stand By Your Man" was what Hillary referred to) protested to the media, "I resent Hillary Clinton's remarks and I want her to know she owes me an apology for what she said."

In a fax she reportedly sent to the Clinton campaign headquarters, she wrote:

"Mrs. Clinton, you have offended every woman and man who loves that song—several million in number.

"How dare you! With all that is in me, I resent your caustic remark. You have offended every true country music fan and every person 'who has made it on their own' with no one to take them to a White House.

"I would like you to appear with me on any forum, including networks, cable, or talk shows and stand toe to toe with me. I can assure you, in spite of your education, you will find me to be just as bright as yourself.

"I will not stand by and allow you or any other person to embarrass, humiliate, and degrade me on national television and print without hearing from me."

While it could be argued that Hillary could learn something from the country music star, she was quick to issue an apology: "I didn't mean to hurt Tammy Wynette as a preson. I happen to be a country-western fan. If she feels like I've hurt her feelings, I'm sorry about that."

The Clintons second strike during the campaign happened just before the New Hampshire primary when the *Wall Street Journal* broke a story about Bill's draft-dodging, which he had before managed to hedge around. While the public wasn't quick to judge him on his moral character, this issue brought up problems with his honesty and integrity. Fortunately, most could sympathize with his fancy maneuverings, since the Vietnam War was never a popular move.

Then came strike three: Whitewater. On March 8, 1992, Jeff Gerth, an investigative reporter for the *New York Times*, ran a story detailing his preliminary investigation into this failed land development corporation and the rather shady dealings the Clintons were involved in. The story cautiously pointed out that the Clintons had entered into a real estate joint venture with a former aide, the late James McDougal, a venture that was at times subsidized by McDougal's failing savings and loan association, Madison Guaranty. Gerth questioned "whether a governor should be involved in a business deal with the owner of a business regulated by the state and whether, having done so, the governor's wife through her law firm should be receiving legal fees for work done for the business."

Gerth illustrated a further possible conflict of interest (or, in Arkansas, politics as usual) involving Hillary: "After Federal regulators found that Mr. McDougal's savings institution, Madison Guaranty, was insolvent, meaning it faced possible closure by the state, Mr. Clinton appointed a new state securities commissioner, who had been a lawyer in a firm that represented the savings and loan. Mr. Clinton and the commissioner deny giving any preferential treatment. The new commissioner approved two novel proposals to help the savings and loan that were offered by Hillary Clinton, Governor Clinton's wife and a lawyer. She and her firm had been retained to represent the association."

Somehow, the Clintons managed to avoid the three-strike rule of political campaigns. Fortunately, Gerth's article was difficult to follow, as was the whole tangled Whitewater web in general. Nonetheless, the article infuriated Hillary, who, according to Stewart in *Blood Sport*, "argued that Gerth was a pawn of the *Times*'s Washington bureau chief, Howell Raines." Stewart writes that Hillary "was convinced that Raines was out to get Clinton because he was jealous of a fellow Southerner his own age who was a serious contender for president." Despite Hillary's somewhat childish desire to launch an attack on the *New York Times*, deputy campaign manager George Stephanopoulos was able to convince her otherwise.

Bill Clinton managed to stave off the media with a few denials and by saying they lost over $25,000 on the deal, although the exact amount seemed to change with each denial. After a minor flurry, and rarely in the headlines, the media remained fairly uninterested. Even so, Gerth's article irritated Hillary to no end, and she commented to a *Newsweek* reporter in a fit of youthful angst, "What's really terrible is finding out that things your father told you are true. He used to tell me, 'Hillary, don't ever forget two things about the establishment: it hates change, and it will always protect its prerogatives.'" Fortunately for the Clintons, that lamentation bore itself out through the Arkansas years, with the good old boys' establishment carrying the Clintons down the path that would lead them to the presidency.

The Clintons were also fortunate that George Bush's son, Jeb, also had questionable dealings with a savings and loan, so he wasn't about to raise the issue in his campaign. Politicians who dared to comment on any improprieties fell victim to a remarkable performance, where the Clintons managed to hide behind one another. Democratic contender Jerry Brown deigned to suggest that Whitewater was "the kind of conflict of interest that is incompatible with the kind of public servant that we expect as president." In his scathing comeback, Bill fumed, "Let me tell you something, Jerry. I don't care what you say about me...but you ought to be ashamed of yourself for jumping on my wife." While Hillary prided herself on being an equal member of a presidential team, suddenly she was back to being a poor little wife, who shouldn't have to be held responsible for her past indiscretions. At the same time, Bill was able to pin the blame on her, in effect neutralizing any possible attack.

Not just a wife for long, though! The day after Bill's defense, Hillary acerbicly fielded NBC reporter Andrea Mitchell's questions about possible improprieties in representing Madison Guaranty before a state agency with, "I suppose I could have stayed home and baked cookies, and had teas." Although she made the remark without thinking, it was an accidental stroke of genius. It created more of a furor than the actual situation.

At this point, members of the campaign committee were beginning to have second thoughts about Hillary exuding such a strong personality, and worried that she might overshadow her husband. In his biography of Bill and Hillary Clinton, George Carpozi, Jr. related the following conversation between Hillary and campaign manager James Carville during the presidential primaries:

"I think you'd better be laid-back for a while," James Carville told Hillary with unaccustomed bluntness. "I have to bring up what Richard Nixon said about you."

"That fink! What did Tricky Dick have to say about me?" Hillary demanded to know.

"He looks upon you and Bill as co-candidates," Carville replied. "And he said that you, being a strong wife, make your husband look like a wimp."

"He said that!"

"That's not all he said. He also said, 'Hillary pounds on the piano so hard that Bill can't be heard.' And his last word on the subject is, 'You want a wife who's intelligent, but not too intelligent.'"

Before Hillary could find her tongue, Carville put in the final word.

"Hillary, you just bug off and lay low. If you don't, you'll have to be satisfied with just being the *first lady* of Arkansas. Period."

And, in seeming apology to her tea and cookies comment, Hillary participated in a *Family Circle* bake-off with Barbara Bush. Even so, Hillary managed to greatly offend the reigning

Eyes on the Presidency

First Lady.

In the May 1992 issue of *Vanity Fair*, Hillary suggested in an interview with Gail Sheehy that the press should look into rumors of extramarital affairs involving George Bush.

When confronted with this information on "NBC Nightly News," Mrs. Bush cried out against the rumors. "The day we start letting lies run a campaign, instead of talking about the issues, is the day we're in sad shape. And I think the press ought to shape up right now."

In that same interview, Mrs. Bush also criticized the media for their handling of the Gennifer Flowers affair:

"I said that about the other sleaze issue, too. I thought it was outrageous that people printed what a woman got paid to say. I thought that was terrible. And I think the press ought to pull themselves up and look at what they're doing and behave themselves. They are taking the campaign and putting it on a level that it should not be."

President Bush also showed his outrage, refusing to even answer any "sleaze questions."

Apparently realizing how unpopular her tabloid-like accusations were, Hillary showed her contrition in the *New York Post*: "Nobody knows better than I how painful discussions of rumors can be. I wouldn't want anybody else, and I certainly don't want the Bush family, subjected to that." She also tried to make herself look better by saying that she had discussed these rumors in a "private conversation." Most people would hardly consider an interview in *Vanity Fair* a private conversation.

SHE TOOK A VILLAGE

Despite little public outcries against Hillary's rude comments, she did mastermind a successful campaign for her husband, cleaning up the messes he had left behind. Together, they won the prize. They would later discover that, unlike the Arkansas press, the national media doesn't allow certain shady dealings to go unnoticed.

Notes on Chapter 4

Page 52. Osborne, Claire G., ed. *The Unique Voice of Hillary Rodham Clinton: A Portrait in Her Own Words*, New York: Avon Books, 1997.

Page 52. Woodward, Bob. *The Agenda: Inside the Clinton White House*, New York: Simon & Schuster, 1994.

Page 53. Stewart, James B. *Blood Sport: The President and His Adversaries*, New York: Simon & Schuster, 1996.

Page 55. Frost, David. Interview. 1992.

Page 55. *Glamour.*

Page 56. Carpozi, George, Jr. *Clinton Confidential: The Climb to Power.*

Page 57. Carpozi, George, Jr. *Clinton Confidential.*

Page 59. "The Numb and the Restless." *The Washington Post.*

Page 59. *The Tonight Show.*

Page 59. Osborne, Claire G., ed. *The Unique Voice of Hillary Rodham Clinton.*

Page 60. Carpozi, George, Jr. *Clinton Confidential.*

Page 60. *USA Today.*

Page 61. *New York Times.*

Page 61. *Star.*

Page 61. Stewart, James B. *Blood Sport.*

Page 62. Kroft, Steve. *60 Minutes.*

Page 63. Carpozi, George, Jr. *Clinton Confidential.*

Page 64. *Wall Street Journal.*

Page 65. Gerth, Jeff. "Clintons Joined S&L Operater in an Ozark Real Estate Venture," *New York Times*, March 8, 1992.

Page 66. Stewart, James B. *Blood Sport.*

Page 66. *Newsweek.*

Page 67. Mitchell, Andrea. *NBC.*

Page 68. Carpozi, George, Jr. *Clinton Confidential.*

Page 68. *Family Circle.*

Page 69. *Vanity Fair*, May 1992.

Page 69. *NBC Nightly News.*

Page 69. *New York Post.*

Page 69.*Vanity Fair.*

5

Mrs. President

For some reason, one of the things Hillary became most known for was her sense of fashion. The media developed an odd fetish for reporting on Hillary's stylistic statements. Why, in an "enlightened" world where women can be known more for their accomplishments than their looks, would Hillary's appearance matter so much? Perhaps because she changed it an average of every month and a half.

As R. Emmett Tyrrell, Jr. recounts in *Boy Clinton*, Hillary's wardrobe designer, Sarah Phillips declared, "There are more pressing things for her to do than dress up like Vogue." Not long after that remark, Hillary showed her "bedroom eyes" in a glamorous spread in—you guessed it—*Vogue*.

Despite protestations from her and her friends about not caring so much about fashion, Hillary seems to spend a lot of her time pandering to the glamour establishment. In the *London Times* on July 7, 1993, Alice Thomson wrote in a feature, "The first lady has managed to transform her mousy tresses three times in the past six months, leaving even Linda Evangelista appearing frumpy." Her frequent changes in style even sparked a web page on the internet entirely devoted to Hillary's hair! To boot, her hair actually ignited a downright controversy, when she charged *Family Circle* $2,000 for her hair stylist's services for a photo shoot.

Hillary became known for other petty actions, as well. Tyrrell writes, "Another row erupted over Rodham's use of a military plane to fly her to Philadelphia on a personal matter, and there was the characteristically mean and dissembling way she paid for the trip upon being caught. She promised to pay the $390 she would have had to pay for a seat on a commercial flight. As for the $4,000 an hour that the military plane actually cost, again the public could be duped; the press would remain indulgent, ignoring even the impudence of her deception."

But money wasn't the only controversial item in Hillary's design to mix her personal life with politics. She had favors to return. Tyrrell continues, "Rodham fired an usher supposedly for talking to Mrs. George Bush, but really because the Clintons cannot conceive of any position not being political and reserved for one of their politically reliable cronies. Her mistrustfulness ignited other rows. The distinguished White House chef got the boot, allegedly for infusing massive doses of cholesterol in the health-crazed First Family's diet."

Hillary became well-known for her contribution to the unemployment rate in Washington. Her unethical firing of the entire White House Travel Office staff gained national attention in the media. Her staff terminations also took a turn for the paranoid. Tyrrell writes, "A [1996] memo by ex-White House aide David Watkins revealed what had long been rumored—Rodham and Clinton's early mistrust of their White House Secret Service detail provoked them to order that the entire detail be fired to be replaced by agents who 'were loyal.'"

While it is traditional for First Ladies to add their special touch to the White House, Hillary's touch fell prey to controversy. Tyrrell points out, "There was a transient row over Rodham's appalling redecoration of the White House, which took a macabre turn when Vince Foster's reputed suicide note claimed that White House ushers 'plotted' to inflate the cost of that redecoration. They had ballooned 60 percent."

In the swarm of controversies surrounding the First Lady, even Christmas couldn't be left alone. In a move against tradition, Hillary dumped Hallmark, which had made Christmas cards for the White House for fifty years. Lois Romano, in her December 3, 1993 *Washington*

Post article, "The Clintons' House of Cards," reported that Hillary had commissioned local artist Susan Davis to paint a watercolor, and that "Davis chose to paint the Truman Balcony, and was then asked to put Socks in, take Socks out, paint the front of the house instead, lighten the sky and darken the sky. Two color sketches, four watercolors and countless work-hours later, Davis was told the Clintons were now considering a plain photo of the White House instead."

Hillary wasn't satisfied with the small controversies surrounding a First Lady, however. She had her heart set on a room with a view. It's traditional for the First Lady to take an office in the East Wing of the White House, away from the center of power and near the social offices. Not one to stand on tradition, however, Hillary demanded a West Wing office, near the business and policy offices and the Oval Office. Several close associates had tried to talk her out of a West Wing office, but she would have none of it. This move would keep her closer to the action and help her to push her own agenda.

A *Washington Post* article said about Hillary, "She has goals, but they appear to be so huge and so far-off—grand and noble things twinkling in the distance—that it's hard to see what she sees...[as she] floats comfortably above the fray of day-to-day Washington." While this highly romanticizes her position, Hillary's goals were grandiose, such as her incredibly inflated health care reform package. With her position of power, and with her ability to hide behind her title of "only" First Lady, it is more apt to say that she floated comfortably above the accountability of day-to-day Washington.

Now that she had her room at the hub of things, Hillary got her hands into everything, including picking her husband's staff. Tyrrell relates in *Boy Clinton*, "As soon as the 1992 election was behind the Clintons, Rodham reverted to her role as public figure. To the usual accompaniment of brass and timpani she became a powerful headhunter for the administration, becoming so much a part of the process that she actually sat in on interviews of prospective nominees."

Her insistence on gender quotas became stifling. One example of this was her insistence on a woman attorney general. A fine goal, indeed, but her nominees got bogged down in the Nannygate crisis. Tyrrell notes that "her quotas also presented the administration with an early morale problem, as seasoned men were passed over or allowed to tread water while Bush holdovers stayed in place for months, then years." He adds, "The administration's abrupt shift leftward away from the centrism of the campaign was another deleterious consequence of Rodham's role as headhunter."

Hillary's first act in helping to choose the cabinet was to suggest 51-year-old Donna Shalala for the post of secretary of Health and Human Services. Ms. Shalala was president of Hunter College in New York, and also served as an assistant secretary of the Department of Housing and Urban Development during the

Carter administration. She didn't have a health policy background, but had been responsible for a 488-bed teaching hospital with a $260 million annual budget. Health care reform advocates expressed concerns about her relative lack of hands-on experience in the field.

In the July 14, 1993 edition of "Review & Outlook," The *Wall Street Journal* voiced concerns about who really runs the White House, noting that "the evidence so far is that control [of the Justice Department] has in fact rested with appointees from Little Rock's Rose Law Firm, which happens to be Hillary Rodham Clinton's former firm." For example, Mr. Clinton conferred with former Rose Law partner Webster Hubbell (then nominated to be associate attorney general) over the Waco crisis, when the obvious choice would have been to consult attorney general Janet Reno.

During the transition, Hillary thought about being Bill Clinton's chief of staff, but was ultimately convinced that it would be a bad idea. Instead, Thomas "Mack" McLarty was chosen for the job. This suited Hillary just fine, since she was close enough to him to maintain some control.

Hillary's Rose Law Firm pal, Vince Foster, got the job as deputy White House counsel. The third of the Rose Law triumvirate, Webster "Web" Hubbell was chosen to run the Justice department during the interim attorney general selection period. Bernard Nussbaum, a well-to-do friend of Hillary's since they served on the House Judiciary Committee during the Watergate investigation, was selected as counsel to the president. In *Blood Sport: The President and His Adversaries*, James Stewart describes a scene where Nussbaum and Foster sit down to discuss anything in their pasts that might embarrass their employers. Nussbaum came up with the fact that "he was a rich mergers lawyer, a fat cat, a product of the 1980s, the very kind of person the Clinton campaign had excoriated." (Never mind that the Clintons themselves were the very kind of people their campaign excoriated.) Foster delivered a very different, eyebrow-raising answer: "There will be rumors of an affair with Hillary." Foster told Nussbaum that "during the campaign, there had even been a press inquiry along that line. He'd been so nervous about it that he'd had his home phone number changed and stayed away from his office for several days to avoid any press calls."

His denials of having an affair with Hillary didn't convince many journalists, among them George Carpozi and David Brock. In *Clinton Confidential*, Carpozi raised questions about exactly what Hillary and Vince were up to on their retreats together at the Rose Law Firm's Ozark Mountains "cabin in the sky." In the January 1994 edition of *The American Spectator*, David Brock set out to unveil Bill Clinton's adulteries with interviews of various Arkansas state troopers who were employed not only to guard the Clintons, but apparently also to serve them in any way possible. In his exposé, Brock relates interviews with various troopers, including Larry Patterson and Roger Perry, who not only revealed Bill's indiscretions, but also a few of Hillary's—with Vince. Brock writes, "According to all of the troopers, whenever Clinton left town, no sooner would he be out of the mansion gates than Foster would appear, often staying in the residence with Hillary into the wee hours of the morning." Off the record, one trooper mentioned he "drove Hillary and Foster to a mountain cabin in Heber Springs, maintained by the Rose firm as an out-of-town retreat for its lawyers, where the two spent significant amounts of time alone."

Patterson and Perry admitted that they once saw Vince and Hillary in a car stopped at a light in Hot Springs "embracing and open-mouth kissing." The troopers also related an incident at Alouette's, a French restaurant in Little Rock, where Foster was seen grabbing various parts of Hillary's anatomy at the bar.

If these allegations are true, who can fault her for trying to seek some of the happiness her husband was enjoying?

Hillary gained an inside to political power with her husband's choice to keep former Rose Law partners Vincent Foster and William Kennedy III in the White House counsel's office. Keeping things in the family, Foster's sister, Sheila Foster Anthony, was nominated to run the Justice Department's legislative office.

Kennedy was responsible for asking the FBI to investigate the White House travel office in the infamous "travelgate," where the travel staff were fired to make way for friends of the Clintons.

The *Wall Street Journal* notes: "She also handpicked old friend Bernard Nussbaum for the top White House counsel position, so in a sense the entire counsel's office reports to her, if not officially at least informally."

Hillary also nominated her old Wellesley roomie, Eleanor Acheson, for chief judge picker. Her friend and co-worker from the Children's Defense Fund, Gerald Torres, was chosen to run the environmental crimes division. Lani Guinier, an old friend of Hillary's, was chosen to fill the civil rights post.

To the surprise of many, the Clintons fired all 32 U.S. attorneys from the Justice Department. Many surmised this was an effort to remove Jay Stephens, who was investigating the House Post Office scandal, which involved House Ways and Means Chairman Dan Rostenkowski.

Interestingly, the U.S. attorney in Little Rock was replaced by Paula Casey, a friend of Hillary and Bill.

The Clintons obviously set the stage to help cover up whatever they saw coming. Surely they knew what to expect, considering Clinton had already been through five elections for governor. With each election, he faced questions about issues ranging from his draft-dodging past to Whitewater. But that was Arkansas, where the media and any other interested persons were quick to forgive and forget. What better way to continue the party than to bring Arkansas to Washington? With all the political maneuvering in such an important department, it leaves us wondering, "Is there any truth in Justice?"

With all the controversy surrounding Bill Clinton's nomination of Webster Hubbell as associate attorney general, Hillary's choices to pack the cabinet can be seen as an effort to maintain some sort of liberal badge on the White House. Hubbell, a former mayor of Little Rock, apparently belonged to a country club that admitted no black members until recently (good thing the Clintons made a big deal out of filling various minority and women quotas when appointing the cabinet). Not that anybody accused Hubbell of racism outright, but it was definitely a liberal hypocrisy that came back to haunt the Clintons. In the late 1980s, Democrat Senators Paul Simon and Howard Metzenbaum used the all-white country club argument to block various Republican nominees. All Simon had to say about Clinton's choice was, "Ideally, I would have preferred that he not belong to a club that has not been admitting blacks."

Hillary's choices were an interesting lot. Lani Guinier (the nominee for the civil rights post) wanted to Balkanize the U.S. by race. Gerald Torres, nominee for environmental crimes, didn't seem to care much for property rights. Two of Bill Clinton's other nominees are also somewhat odd choices. Walter Dellinger, nominee for office of legal counsel, supported Congressional claims in the '80s, even though this position is supposed to protect the power of the president. Drew Days, nominee for solicitor general, subscribes to what the *Wall Street Journal* calls "the Larry Tribe school of exotic legal activism."

No wonder the Clintons were widely accused of "politicizing" Justice!

The *Wall Street Journal* comments in its May 12, 1993 "Review & Outlook" column: "These nominees are 'political' not because they are friends with a President but in a much more dangerous sense. They're the sort of law school professors/activists who want to visit their strange theories on the rest of us. This seems to be the legal-political community that advises Hillary, and we suspect Bill felt obliged to name such people to appease his party's left. And that he expects Mr. Hubbell to temper their activism with political reality; someone has to provide adult supervision."

Fortunately, Reno managed to get her own pick, Jo Ann Harris, to run Justice's criminal division. Not without a fight, however; she had to fight Hillary's friend, Susan Thomases, who tried to get her law partner, Benito Romano, into that position. Perhaps this was a concession on the Clinton's part to appease those who accused them of "cronyism." Certainly this label couldn't apply to two people who had accused Ronald Reagan of cronyism because of his choice to appoint Ed Meese as attorney general.

The issue of Health Care Reform raised the question of what Hillary and her cronies were doing in the Oval Office.

In July of 1992, Hillary Clinton said, "I'd

like to think of ways to open up the White House." But the question remained, open up the White House to whom?

As Bob Woodward writes in *The Agenda*, Hillary was Bill Clinton's most important advisor. She would only be content with a senior post in the White House, and had originally wanted to be the top domestic policy advisor. Clinton's inner circle were worried that this "would be politically explosive, send the wrong message, and invite attention and Lady Macbeth stories about her as the true source of Clinton's ambition and drive."

Instead, they did what had worked in Arkansas: they gave her a project to supervise, which gave her the chance to install her cronies in official positions. In Arkansas it was education reform; in Washington, they handed her health care reform. Her cronies came with the deal. Happy with her new appointment, Hillary rolled up her sleeves.

Ah, the road to the White House is paved with good intentions and forgotten promises! During the all-important New Hampshire primaries, the presidential candidates offered their various health care plans. As outlined in *The Comeback Kid* by Charles F. Allen and Jonathan Portis, Bill Clinton's plan would include:

Every American having access to health care, to be paid for by sweeping insurance reform. His plan would end "the administrative waste of the current system, control the unnecessary spread of excessive technology, stop drug prices from going up at three times the rate of inflation, reduce billing fraud that may account for up to $75 billion a year and force the people who send bills and the people who pay them to agree on how much health care should cost."

Increased children's access to health care, including putting clinics in schools.

Increased primary and preventive care in inner-city and rural areas.

Improved senior citizen care. According to Clinton, "Our senior citizens should make their own choices about how to spend their health care benefits. In Arkansas, we created a program that gives seniors the right to take money which used to be used...for nursing home care and spend it on home health care, personal care, transportation to senior centers, hiring a nurse or attending an adult day care center. I want a federal health system that gives seniors all over the country the same choices."

Fitting these high ideals into a specific package, however, proved to be too much for the Clinton administration to handle. Technically, of course, the mastermind of the whole health care reform package wasn't part of the Clinton administration. Hillary couldn't hold a high-level appointed position because of the "Bobby Kennedy Law," or the Federal Salary Act of 1967. This was enacted to prevent a situation that occurred during the Kennedy administration, when President John F. Kennedy appointed his brother, Robert F. Kennedy, as attorney general.

Since Hillary took no salary for her efforts, she didn't fall under this law. Apparently, it's not considered nepotism if you don't get paid for it.

According to Bob Woodward, in his book *The Agenda*, an insider's look at the first year of the Clinton presidency, Clinton's inner circle decided to give Hillary a project to get her out of their hair. Thus, she was put in charge of the health care task force, which grew to over 500 members.

Reportedly due to leaks to the media, Hillary closed up the same White House she had said she wanted to open. She held the health care task force meetings in private.

On March 10, 1993, the federal courts ruled that "one of the first actions taken by the president [the secret meetings] was in violation of the [government access law]." Hillary was forced to make the meetings public, and the public began to worry when they caught a glimpse of her plans. As Kevin H. Watson writes in *The Clinton Record*, "Visions of a federal health care system, with the efficiency of the Post Office and the compassion of the Internal Revenue Service began to break up support for the Clinton's plans."

To make matters worse, government auditors later found that this task force that originally had a budget of a few hundred thousand dollars had spent over 13 million dollars. That would have been just the beginning for a health care program that would have been destined to experience severe cost overruns.

In his usual lambasting the left style, political commentator Rush Limbaugh brings up some interesting points in his book, *See, I Told You So*. He asks, "Do you think that if the

Clinton campaign had told the American people the truth in 1992 about its intentions for health care that Bill Clinton could have won the election? Imagine if they told us that Hillary was going to select a health-care task force of some 524 people that nobody will know, nobody will ever see, that no doctors or insurance people will be a part of the team, that meetings will beheld in secret, and that the result could well be a payroll tax increase. How would that program have fared with the public? There is no way Clinton would have been elected. Instead, the Clinton campaign consistently denied that Hillary would have any special power or authority."

The clincher on this issue is that the Clintons turned health care into a crisis, when America arguably has the best health care system in the world. Nations such as Russia, China and East European countries are trading in their socialized health care systems for models that more closely resemble the United States.

Hillary cited a statistic that 37 million Americans don't have health insurance. This figure is misleading, because a 1990 Census Bureau study found that the long-term uninsured were fewer than 10 million. A Congressional Budget Office study showed that about half of those without insurance found coverage within four months, and 72 percent were covered within one year. In addition, those without insurance still had access to health care through emergency rooms, often with financial assistance from the health care institution.

Hillary also excoriated the pharmaceuticals industry for ripping off the public with their greedy profiteering. Never mind that pharmaceutical companies have developed all kinds of miracle drugs, helping to raise the American life expectancy. Never mind that several companies have programs to provide free prescription drugs to families with an income of $35,000 or less.

Unfortunately, the best way to increase health care costs is to put the government in control. Just look at the sky-high tax rates in countries with socialized medicine if you're in doubt. Closer to home, take Medicare as an example of government-controlled health care. At its implementation in 1965, when it cost taxpayers about $3 billion per year, experts estimated it would cost $9 billion by 1990. The actual cost for 1990 was $67 billion! Add to this the fact that the baby-boom generation is heading towards retirement, leaving a narrower tax base to cover health care costs. Our grandchildren's children will be paying our bills.

Notes on Chapter 5

Page 73. Tyrrell, R. Emmett, Jr. *Boy Clinton: The Political Biography*, Washington, D.C.: Regnery Publishing, Inc., 1996.

Page 74. *Vogue.*

Page 74. Thomson, Alice. *London Times*, July 7, 1993.

Page 74. *Family Circle.*

Page 74. Tyrrell, R. Emmett, Jr. *Boy Clinton.*

Page 75. Tyrrell, R. Emmett, Jr. *Boy Clinton.*

Page 75. Romano, Lois. "The Clintons' House of Cards," *Washington Post*, December 3, 1993.

Page 76. *Washington Post.*

Page 77. Tyrrell, R. Emmett, Jr. *Boy Clinton.*

Page 78. "Review & Outlook," *Wall Street Journal*, July 14, 1993.

Page 79. Stewart, James B. *Blood Sport: The President and His Adversaries*, New York: Simon & Schuster, 1996.

Page 79. Carpozi, George, Jr. *Clinton Confidential: The Climb to Power.*

Page 79. Brock, David. *The American Spectator*, January 1994.

Page 81. *Wall Street Journal.*

Page 83. *Wall Street Journal.*

Page 83. "Review & Outlook."

Page 84. Woodward, Bob. *The Agenda: Inside the Clinton White House*, New York: Simon & Schuster, 1994.

Page 84. Allen, Charles F. and Jonathan Portis. *The Comeback Kid: The Life and Career of Bill Clinton*, New York: Carol Publishing Group, 1992.

Page 86. Woodward, Bob. *The Agenda.*

JHE TOOK A VILLAGE

Page 86. Watson, Kevin H. *The Clinton Record: Everything Bill and Hillary Want You to Forget!* Bellevue, Washington: Merril Press, 1996.

Page 86. Limbaugh, Rush. *See, I Told You So.*

6

Whitewater

In the *Unique Voice of Hillary Rodham Clinton* appears this classic quote by Hillary: "I'm concerned about who will enter public life, who will stay in public life, the quality of decisions that are made, the extraordinary role that big moneyed interests will play because they can marshal information-driven campaigns that permeate the atmosphere with misinformation or, if not wrong information, [information that is] inaccurate because [it is] incomplete."

As the incredible potpourri of deals, steals, lies and cover-ups the media lumped together under the label "Whitewater" reveals, Hillary spoke with the voice of experience. In a way, it should be reassuring that the Clintons have fallen prey to the same capitalist "greed" they have so heartily denounced. Yet their means for acquiring the wealth they so desperately coveted would leave even the greatest of this century's early robber barons taking notes. From closet socialist to closet capitalist, Hillary has once again shown how her political agenda easily changes to suit her needs.

Coming from comparatively modest backgrounds, the Clintons themselves wouldn't be considered "big moneyed interests" (although, as is discussed later in this chapter, there is a good chance they have more than they say they do), but they sure knew how to wheel and deal with the big boys in Arkansas. And, as uncovered during their second term, they took wheeling and dealing to an art form with not only national, but international, bigwigs as well. Hillary proved herself an expert in befriending those who could bring her to power, and showed she was not adverse to using her cronies for a little personal enrichment.

Whitewater. A romantic name for some 230 acres of land located along the White River in the Ozarks of Arkansas. An apt name for a controversy so tangled and bungled that it is difficult to decide where one debacle begins and another ends. More importantly, it is so difficult to unravel that it may be well into the next century before investigations reveal exactly which laws were broken, and when. There is no doubt that laws *were* broken, and there is no doubt that the Clintons and their friends have used the subterfuge of elapsed time and "lost" documents to their full advantage.

Whitewater

"Whitewater" is a term used loosely to describe a series of fiascos and shady dealings the Clintons were involved in during the 1980s and beyond. More particularly, they involved Hillary, since she generally handled the family finances (Bill, although a Rhodes Scholar and Yale Law graduate, had little mind for business and money). Whitewater covers a whole realm of potential political abuses, including land deals by the Whitewater Development Corporation (partly owned by the Clintons), the failure of Madison Guaranty Savings and Loan, Hillary's extraordinarily excellent adventures in the stock market, possible conflicts of interest between Hillary's law firm and her involvement in state affairs, and the various cover-ups and timely coincidences that have thrown investigators off the track.

Reporter Meredith L. Oakley tracked the Clintons for thirteen years, beginning with their days as governor and first lady of Arkansas. She had many conversations with Bill Clinton during that time, and learned Bill's strategy. She notes that one of his most troubling traits is his "ability to appear to be great without actually being so." As the backbone beneath his campaigns and his presidency, however, Hillary has shown her greatness both in her ability to maneuver politics to suit her needs and in her shrewd financial sense. While the Clintons claimed they lost money on the whole Whitewater affair, evidence points to a possible financial gain in the hundreds of thousands of dollars, not to mention political gain for themselves and their friends.

JHE TOOK A VILLAGE

The Clintons chose well in deciding to wait until 1992 to run for president. Since character was not an issue during that campaign (the public had apparently had enough during the tribulations of the 1988 candidates), the Clintons managed to sidestep issues such as Bill's womanizing, "not inhaling" marijuana use, draft-dodging, and conflicts of interest. The media basically left it to the tabloids to exploit these issues, and beyond the preliminary titillation, the public shrugged its shoulders and the Clintons were able to move on.

Then the press began to seriously look into a small, money-losing venture called the Whitewater Development Corporation. Ms. Oakley provides a good reason why Whitewater initially raised eyebrows. She writes: "Hillary may have been bored by the teas-and-cookies role assigned by the public to [Arkansas's] first ladies, but it served her personal interests well. She was able to ply her lawyer's trade and manage the couple's investment portfolio without public scrutiny of any sort. Indeed, no one was more surprised than the Arkansas news media when revelations about Hillary's involvement in Whitewater-Madison began surfacing in late 1993. Clinton's foibles were well known and even accepted in his home state; Hillary's were not."

The Clintons have managed to keep themselves surprisingly clean during investigations. Even with allegations flying left and right, they succeeded in winning a second term. Hillary has been able to shrug off accusations, demurely claiming ignorance of the kind of people she was working with and what they were up to. It's amazing how quickly she can go from professional go-getter to "I'm just a girl." It's impossible to believe that she had no idea what she was doing.

It all started with the late Jim McDougal, a man who apparently reveled in walking on the edge. As a professor at Ouachita Baptist University in Arkadelphia, Arkansas, he met and started dating Susan Henley, a nineteen-year-old beauty queen contestant and student. Fifteen years her senior, he continued dating her even after a warning from the university president. Eventually, they married. He drove his public life just as fast and furious as his private life. A master of networking, he managed to make friends with everybody in the Arkansan political realm. It was inevitable that he and Bill should become acquainted.

During Bill's early days working on Senator Fulbright's campaign, Jim took the fledgling politician under his wing, teaching him the proper attire for a political aspirant and introducing him to the right people. He jump-started Bill's campaign for Arkansas attorney general with a $1500 check and a crowd gathered with Susan's help at Bill's first speech. Jim was open with Bill about his membership in Alcoholics Anonymous. What wouldn't be discovered until much later was Jim's devastating personality disorder, manic depression. Jim's exceptionally high energy and drive would give way to periods of severe depression. This man, who, at his best, made a killing in real estate, would lure the Clintons (easy prey for a way to make a quick buck) into becoming partners in the Whitewater Development Corporation. It was all downhill from there.

The fact that the Clintons were able to get a loan to purchase the 230 acres that McDougal insisted would sell at a huge profit demonstrates a little Arkansas-style wheeling and dealing. McDougal decided to get the loan through the Citizens Bank and Trust Co., founded and directed by Chris Wade, who, conveniently, was the real estate broker who alerted McDougal to this hot new deal. Never mind that the president of the bank was James Patterson, one of the investors in 101 Development Corp., who was selling the land. So what if the Clintons were a weak financial risk, at best, and so what if the bank already had a dangerously high concentration of loans granted for that area? In *Blood Sport: The President and His Adversaries*, James Stewart writes, "[Loan officer Frank] Burge discussed his concerns with the bank's board members. They were, of course, aware that Clinton was likely to be the state's next governor....Burge, in particular, thought the presence of Clinton in the deal made it all but a sure thing, assuming Clinton did become governor. He assumed that wealthy Clinton supporters would simply buy the lots at highly inflated prices as a clandestine means of funneling money into the governor's pockets, thereby gaining influence."

Even so, the Clintons were required to put ten percent down on the $200,000 loan. No problem: McDougal would just pull a few strings to get a loan for the down payment from

Union National Bank of Little Rock. Stewart writes, "McDougal and Harry Don Denton, Union Bank's chief loan officer, were friends, Union having handled most of McDougal's earlier ventures with Senator Fulbright, financed a below-market interest rates 'as an accommodation' to the senator, according to the bank's records. Referring to an earlier financial statement submitted by McDougal, the bank cited McDougal's assets as $975,245, liabilities of $424,054, for a net worth of $551,191; for Clinton it listed only unsecured liabilities of $27,211." It helps to have friends in high places; Stewart goes on to mention that the bank gave the Clintons an unsecured loan.

You try getting a $20,000 unsecured loan from a bank with no assets and unsecured liabilities of $27,211. When you get turned down, do you really think Bill and Hillary will feel your pain?

Of course, when one is governor, one can make friends in high places where they didn't previously exist. Watson writes, "Allegations indicate that President Clinton used his position as Governor of Arkansas to not only get a sweet deal in the Whitewater investment, but also to prevent government regulators from shutting down some of the S&Ls in question." He cites an example where Clinton replaced the Arkansas Director of Fish and Wildlife. His new appointee worked out a deal where the Department of Fish and Wildlife would receive land from Whitewater Development Corporation. In return, Fish and Wildlife managed to get the highway department to build an access road to the development property. Fish and Wildlife was also required to build a boat ramp on the piece of property it received.

In his announcement speech for President of the United States, this same man would lament, "The 1980s ushered in a Gilded Age of greed and selfishness, of irresponsibility and of neglect." Let's look at some of that '80s greed and selfishness:

The Clintons claim that they lost money on the Whitewater deal, although the exact amount is questionable: Bill once claimed they lost about $25,000, then later upped it to $40,000, and then Denver attorney James Lyons claimed they lost $69,000. Investigations found that the report asserting a loss of $69,000 was flawed, with some key records missing. For some reason, the Clintons did not declare any of these figures as a loss on their tax returns for that period. In fact, they claimed a capital gain of $1,000 for selling their interest in Whitewater back to the McDougals. In an interview with the *Washington Post*, Arkansas real estate agent Chris Wade said he did not believe the real estate venture lost money. The records are so convoluted that they may never be completely deciphered by investigators.

While the Clintons held the power, the McDougals had the money and the know-how. To increase the value of the land they had invested in, Susan McDougal negotiated the foursome through a series of "land flips." Land flips involve selling the same piece of land to various accomplices for increasingly higher prices. This increases the loan amount needed to buy the land, with the artificially raised value of the property more than offsetting increased property taxes.

Mr. Watson gives the following example in *The Clinton Record*: On October 14, 1978, the Clintons and McDougals sold a parcel of the land for $2,000. Watson shows that "the very next day, that same parcel of land was sold again for $32,250. Susan McDougal managed to pull off several of these transactions using financing from a bank called Madison Guaranty Savings and Loan." This ill-fated S&L would become another hot topic in the whole Whitewater affair.

In his tell-all book, *Clinton Confidential: The Climb to Power*, celebrated author and biographer George Carpozi, Jr. sheds more light on the Whitewater deals and steals. He cites several examples of poor people losing a lot of money to the Clintons and McDougals—possibly more money than will ever be uncovered by any investigation into the matter. "The Clintons and McDougals profited enormously in the dozen years of their partnership. They did it by hook and by crook—mostly by crook—and they managed to hide their huge profits in a manner that would have made Al Capone ashamed to call himself a gangster."

Mr. Carpozi got his information from records that Jim McDougal *sold* in April 1994. (He was apparently trying to make even more money off of Whitewater by selling thousands of documents at 50 cents per page!) To the McDougals' (and the Clintons') detriment, these documents, which had most likely been cleaned up at least twice before their release, contained information that prompted the criminal investigation into the affairs of the two couples.

Mr. Carpozi's first example is that of Clyde Soapes, Jr., a not very well-off grain elevator operator. Soapes was possibly drawn in by a Whitewater Development Corporation commercial saying, "Reckon a feller could live off the land here if he was of a mind to...just ten percent down and seven years to pay it off." The deal Soapes ended up with, however, was $3,000 down on a $14,000 parcel of land (a 21% down payment), with $244.69 monthly installments over the next four years—certainly not the deal promised in the ad!

The real clincher in the deal was the Purchase Agreement, a document allowed by Arkansas law to allow people of limited means to buy real estate. With this signed document, a mortgager bypasses a credit check on the purchaser, and in return, the purchaser puts up a large, non-refundable down payment. But that's not all: if even one payment is late, it is considered a default, and the property reverts back to the mortgager. Yet, according to Mr. Carpozi, there was no bona fide warning to the purchaser about what would happen to the deal if payments weren't made when due.

Soapes, who had met 35 of the 48 installments and was less than $2,500 away from owning the property, fell ill with diabetes. He notified Whitewater Development Corporation to explain his situation, asking for an extension. In response, the company sent him a notice that he had defaulted on his loan, but they would be happy to sell the property to him (again) with $3,000 down and 48 monthly payments of $244.69.

This, from a governor whose running platform included consumer advocacy! This, from a governor and first lady wanting to make Arkansas live up to its state slogan as being the Land of Opportunity. It certainly was the Land of Opportunity for those in power.

Soapes was only one of hundreds of other buyers who signed Purchase Agreements with Whitewater Development Corporation. And look what happened to just this one piece of property:

Soapes was not able to set up another Purchase Agreement with Whitewater Development, and the $11,564.15 in payments he had made was unrecoverable. (Soapes died three years later, in 1990). The Clintons and McDougals resold Soapes's property to another couple, who signed a Purchase Agreement to buy the land for $18,000. They made $16,500 in payments, missed a month in early 1990, and lost the land—and their money. A third buyer lost the land after making $6,400 in payments. The fourth and final buyer finally managed to buy the land for about $20,000. The Clintons and McDougals made $63,000 on this parcel of land that was originally worth $14,000.

One more word about the Purchase Agreements buyers signed with Whitewater Development: there were no county records of Soapes' transaction. The reason? Because of the default, no title passed hands. Since there was no title, there was also no trace of the transaction to report to the IRS. Multiplying this type of deal by the hundreds of parcels processed by Whitewater Development Corporation, it is easy to extrapolate that the Clintons and McDougals possibly have up to five million dollars in a secret stash somewhere.

Mr. Carpozi cites Bruce May, an Arizona real estate lawyer and chairman of an American Bar Association committee on land sale regulation: "That is clearly not a very consumer-oriented method of selling [land] at all." May goes on to say that "You couldn't get away with that in Arizona or, I believe, in most other states. It's common for states to protect purchasers from these kind of agreements."

Carpozi quotes one person from the Arkansas Real Estate Commission as saying, "Quite frankly, we received very few, if any, complaints about Purchase Agreements—and we have absolutely no record of a single complaint against Whitewater Development."

Of course—Governor Clinton was responsible for appointing the members of the Real Estate Commission to their seats!

Another arm of the Whitewater affair involves the Madison Guaranty Savings & Loan scandal. In a speech castigating President Bush in October 1991, Clinton said, "When the rip-off artists looted our S&L's, the President was silent. In the Clinton administration, when people sell their companies and their workers and their country down the river, they'll get called on the carpet."

How true! Of course, it's not so fun when it's the accuser who's standing on that carpet.

Whitewater

While the Clintons may not have personally ripped off Madison Guaranty, they made it possible for others to do so in a brilliant scheme to "save" the S&L. Many ethics issues have been raised over this S&L scandal. The essential question is whether then Governor Clinton used his office to keep Madison alive while friends and acquaintances robbed it to the tune of $47 to $60 million at taxpayers' expense.

Journalist Jeff Gerth brought up the Madison issue in the *New York Times* during the 1992 campaign, but it was swiftly squelched by Denver attorney James Lyons before reaching controversy proportions. Then, in 1993, two things happened. The S&L clean-up and investigative organization, the Resolution Trust Corp., referred Madison for criminal investigation. The second trigger came with the indictment of former Judge David Hale, a Clinton pal who said he had made a loan that was partly responsible for the failure of Capital-Management Services Inc., at Clinton's request.

The Clintons and McDougals, remember, entered the Whitewater venture in 1978. Jim McDougal bought Madison Guaranty in 1979 with a loan from Worthen Bank. Madison held Whitewater's accounts, which were often overdrawn.

According to *The Wall Street Journal*, Madison's assets grew from $6 million in 1982 to $107 million in 1985. Loans to its officers and directors grew from $500,000 to $17 million. Senator Fulbright, for whom both Bill Clinton and Jim McDougal had worked, and other political figures in Arkansas also received loans from Madison. According to the *Los Angeles Times*, Arkansas Governor Jim Guy Tucker (Clinton's successor) worked out a deal with Madison to reduce his debt of over $1 million by 50%.

As an interesting sideline, several questionable campaign contributions originated from a 1985 fund-raiser Jim McDougal held at Madison Guaranty to retire Bill Clinton's 1984 campaign debts. The campaign owed Clinton $50,000, and he in turn owed that amount to another Arkansas bank, which was owned by one of his senior aides. There were several cashier's checks for $3,000 drawn on Madison as donations to the campaign. One was issued in the name of Ken Peacock, the son of one of the directors. When asked about it by the *Washington Post*, he replied, "I don't know anything about it." Was this a way of funneling money to the Clintons at taxpayers' expense?

According to Susan McDougal, the Clintons' partner in the Whitewater deal, Hillary used her power to help save Madison Guaranty Savings & Loan owned by the McDougals. Hillary was one of two lawyers listed as contacts in the initial pleading to the securities commissioner. Susan McDougal said that the Rose Law firm "petitioned the state securities commissioner to approve in principle a plan by Madison to issue preferred stock as a means of acquiring the additional capital to take it out of its bind."

There were many reports that when the securities commissioner wouldn't comply, he was replaced by a new Clinton appointee,

Beverly Bassett Schaffer. Schaffer did approve the scheme, but denied any favoritism to Madison. How can we be sure of that, considering Schaffer had once served as a lawyer for Madison, and Jim McDougal had recommended her appointment? And considering that one of her letters to Madison attorney Hillary Clinton on the matter opened with a rather chummy "Dear Hillary"?

Hillary, by the way, received $2,000 a month as a retainer fee to represent Madison. The *Los Angeles Times* reported that Jim McDougal said he "hired Hillary because Bill came in whimpering they needed help." More Arkansas back-scratching?

David Hale was appointed by then Governor Clinton as the first judge of Arkansas's first municipal claims court. By 1986, Hale ran the largest court in the state, and also headed Capital-Management Services Inc., a small business investment company taken over by the Small Business Administration after a federal grand jury indicted Hale on charges of defrauding the SBA.

Capital-Management Services was permitted to make loans only to socially or economically disadvantaged small businesses. Hale charged that Clinton urged him to make a $300,000 loan from Capital Management to a real estate firm owned by Susan McDougal. Investigators immediately began to wonder if some of this money ended up in Whitewater's accounts.

Hale brought these accusations to light in a plea bargain attempt to reduce his own sentence. The case was being handled by Paula Casey, the U.S. attorney the Clintons assigned to Little Rock after they fired all 32 attorneys in the Justice Department. She agreed with prosecutors early in the case not to follow it, but she later recused herself from Madison-Whitewater, so it could be investigated by those not so close to the President and First Lady.

As *The Wall Street Journal* noted in its December 28, 1993 edition, the facts available in the Madison Guaranty issue "contain no 'smoking gun,' but they surely arouse suspicion. Surely Hillary Clinton was disingenuous in saying during her year-end interview that she is 'bewildered' that Whitewater remains 'a topic of inquiry.'"

The article goes on to mention a situation raising more concerns: "The Clinton Administration has just proposed a sweeping change to give the President much more direct control over regulation of banks throughout the land. Before that happens, at the very least, some of those involved in Whitewater should go up on oath somewhere to testify on what really happened when Bill Clinton presided over banking regulation in Arkansas." We can only hope!

In a plea resounding with overtones of Nixon's "I am not a crook" speech, Bill Clinton said, "I haven't done anything wrong." Perhaps that is because he leaves the dirty work to others? Another topic brought up, but not closely pursued (maybe for good reason), is the string of mysterious deaths and acts of violence that have surrounded the Clintons, as if they were at the eye of an incredibly destructive hurricane.

None of the deaths or acts of violence mentioned here can be directly pinpointed to either of the Clintons. They all seem unrelated, but when taken together, it seems impossible that they could be mere coincidence. The violence surrounding various acquaintances of the Clintons is eerie, reminiscent of past president Lyndon Johnson, who left a similar "trail of bodies" on his way to the White House.

In his book, *Clinton Confidential: The Climb to Power*, George Carpozi, Jr. relates an intriguing series of deaths—perhaps murders—and other acts of violence surrounding the Clintons. Their implications are inconceivable in this "civilized" day and age, especially for a president who claimed to be responsible for putting a disputed additional 100,000 policemen on the streets -- he himself admitted he had fallen short in his 1998 State of the Union message, pleading for more help to finish the job. But consider the following cases:

Journalist L. J. Davis relates his close call with death in an article in the April 4, 1994 edition of *The New Republic*, "An Arkansas Thriller: The Name of Rose." He had traveled to Little Rock, Russellville and Mena to dig deeper into the Whitewater mystery. He must have hit a little too close to home. On Valentine's Day 1994, as he entered his room at the Legacy Hotel in Little Rock, Davis was struck unconscious by a blow to his head. He knew it couldn't have been a robbery, because he still had his watch and cash in his wallet.

Robbery was further ruled out by the

warnings he had received earlier from a Washington contact, who told him, "You've gotten into a red zone." The contact had told him, "Work your ass off and get out of there as fast as possible."

He returned to New York the next day. On March 8, after recovering from his concussion and a blood clot that had formed, Davis sent his article from his computer to *The New Republic* offices. Within three hours, an unidentifiable voice called and told him, "What you're doing makes Lawrence Walsh look like a rank amateur." (Walsh was the Iran-Contra special counsel.)

When Davis asked who the caller was, he received in reply, "Seems to me you've gotten your bell rung too many times....But did you hear what I just said?"

Somebody was obviously on Davis's trail. And they weren't very friendly.

In 1993, reporter David Brock interviewed Arkansas state troopers referred to as "pimps in uniform" for Bill Clinton while he was governor. He sent his initial findings to Wladyslaw Pleszczynski, managing editor of *The American Spectator*. On September 3, Pleszczynski found that the magazine's office had been broken into. It appeared that someone had cut a hole into the mailroom wall, rifled through all the desk drawers, and had taken a boom box and a Sony Walkman. A week later, the office was broken into again, through the same place, after it had been repaired. Apparently, the burglar didn't find what he or she was looking for. Almost two weeks later, someone broke into the magazine's studio apartment in a different location. In its 27 years of operation, the magazine had never had any break-ins. Pleszczynski said, "We didn't necessarily connect them with David Brock's research, but it makes you wonder."

On January 24, 1994, a fire broke out in the offices of the Pete Marwick accounting firm. The White House hired this firm to audit the travel office just before the decision to fire the staff. The Marwick firm had also done an audit on Madison Guaranty Savings & Loan commissioned by Jim McDougal in 1986.

Deroy Murdock, writer and president of Loud & Clear Communications, a marketing and media consulting company, reported in the *New York Post*: "The timing of the blaze seems significant coming just four days after the appointment of Whitewater special prosecutor Robert Fiske and within three days of the Rose Law Firm's reported shredding of documents that belonged to...Vincent Foster."

On Tuesday, July 20, 1993, deputy White House counsel Vincent Foster's body was found at Fort Marcy, Virginia. He was found about 200 yards away from his car, slumped against a cannon, dead from a gunshot wound to his head. There was a gun in his hand.

In his book, *Friends in High Places*, Webb Hubbell, former Rose Law Firm chief operating officer and long-time Clinton confidant, recounts how Vince Foster and Hillary Rodham Clinton met at a 1976 legal aid clinic in Fayetteville: Foster returned to his office in the Rose Law Firm "raving, uncharacteristically, about a smart female law professor he had worked with up there." After facing strong opposition at Rose, Foster was instrumental in aiding Hillary in becoming the firm's first "lady lawyer."

At Rose Law Firm, Foster, Hubbell, and Hillary formed an unprecedented friendship, relying on each other for moral support and companionship. In an atmosphere of dog-eat-dog, their unique friendship would spark gossip that later aroused suspicions of the incidents involving Rose Law Firm.

Life at Rose Law Firm was not all that rosy for Hillary. Being the first lady lawyer at Rose did not immunize Hillary from the rules of proper attire and attitude of a professional. Being one of her closest friends, Foster often took the brunt of the firm's attack on Hillary's mod taste in clothing and her use of her maiden name while Bill Clinton was the newly elected state Attorney General. Although she deferred and took her husband's last name to help Bill's political campaigning, Hubbell recalls how Hillary was deeply hurt that "she was forced to live so far inside her that she sometimes didn't know who she was."

With adjoining offices, Hillary and Foster often worked late into the evenings. Their close work relationship during this time would later spark rumors of an affair that tabloids printed during the 1992 Gennifer Flowers incident.

The rumors of a Hillary and Foster affair were not the only incident that took a toll on their unique friendship. There were also rumors about Hillary, Foster, and Hubbell plotting a takeover of Rose Law Firm. Despite the investigation by the Federal Savings and Loan Insurance Corporation, Hillary, Foster, and Hubbell emerged as dominant partners at Rose, which by then had expenses in the hundred of thousands.

Their relationship deteriorated further during the internal investigation of the White House Travel Office career staff firings. Foster felt that he had caused the mess himself. He felt guilty that Bill Kennedy and David Watkins took the fall for him. Hillary grew cold to Foster and the relationship soured. Hillary became curt and demanding: "Fix it, Vince," "Handle it, Vince." Foster told Hubbell at one of their last dinner meetings, "It's just not the same." A few days later, Foster was dead.

While we are supposed to assume this was a suicide, Foster left behind a wife and three children, to whom he was very devoted. U.S. Park officials found no suicide note. He had no history of depression. Stress would be an unlikely cause, because he was obviously no stranger to stress as a lawyer whose specialty was in litigation. Friends and acquaintances of Foster considered it unlikely that he would commit suicide. Perhaps the pressures of being under such close public scrutiny finally got to him. Did it have something to do with his personal relationship with the First Lady?

Or did it have something to do with the fact that Foster had recently been ordered to take care of the financial documents relating to Whitewater?

If that were so, why then the cover-up? And there were certainly some odd behaviors on the part of the First Lady and White House staff, brushed off with explanations that seemed—well, lame.

As testified by a Secret Service agent, the night after Foster's death, White House Counsel Bernard Nussbaum and one of Hillary's personal aides removed boxes of files from Foster's office. Phone records indicated that the aide had been in contact with Hillary during the night. The aide claimed that they had been looking for a suicide note, and that they hadn't removed any files. In *The Clinton Record*, Kevin Watson sums it up:

"According to Hillary and her aide, this is what we are supposed to believe: The aide had gone home from work for the day and was told about Foster's death by a late night phone call. After a few phone calls with Hillary, the aide decides to go back to the White House. She returns there out of grief, and not under orders from Hillary. The aide happened to be wandering the halls of the White House and went by Foster's office. When she saw a light in the office and went in, she met Bernie Nussbaum. In a moment of grief, she decided to try and look for a suicide note. When she left, she was not carrying any boxes of files as reported by the Secret Service agent. Hmm...."

Clinton's response to the media the day of Foster's death was, "There is really no way to know why these things happen." He added, "We'll just have to live with something else we can't understand."

Whitewater

That's probably true. While this case was turned over to Attorney General Janet Reno and Deputy Attorney General Philip Heymann for investigation, it was interesting that the FBI was in a state of flux, with the forced resignation of FBI Director William Sessions.

Despite calls from the press for a rigorous investigation into the matter, somehow the investigation just kind of fizzled out. Instead of Heymann leading a probe into Foster's death, it was left to U.S. Park Police to handle it as just another routine corpse.

In 1991, Bill Clinton, then governor of Arkansas, contracted with American Contract Services, Inc. to provide private security guards for him to replace the free Secret Service protection he received as a presidential candidate. This security guard service was run by Luther "Jerry" Parks. Mr. Carpozi relates that an insider said Clinton "wanted Parks's guards to be his buffers when he did his screwing on the campaign trail."

Later, Parks started to do research on Clinton's affairs, and uncovered a large amount of information. Mrs. Parks remembers that in mid-September 1993, her house was broken into, and her husband's records on Clinton were stolen. Then on September 26, Luther Parks was murdered, shot with ten bullets from a .9 millimeter, semi-automatic pistol.

In a seemingly unrelated incident, on March 3, 1994, Dr. Ronald Rogers died in a plane crash. The cause was reported as "electrical problems." Upon closer scrutiny, circumstances surrounding Rogers's death are suspicious. Journalist Ambrose Evans-Pritchard had been dispatched by London's *Sunday Telegraph* to dig further into Jerry Parks's murder. He was going to interview Dr. Rogers, who lived close to the cabin owned by Clinton's mother on Lake Hamilton near Hot Springs. Evans-Pritchard, who also experienced other "adventures" during his investigations in Arkansas, reported, "It's a bit difficult for people to understand that this is going on in the borders of the U.S. There's a serious shutting-up operation under way."

Recounting another incident, Mr. Carpozi described a videotape of events at Waco. The videotape includes a scene where three security guards have climbed a ladder to a second-floor roof overhang, where they climb through a window. According to Mr. Carpozi:

"As this trio disappear after going through the window, a fourth agent, having climbed to the roof setback, reaches for one of two grenades dangling from his belt.

"Taking it in hand, he pulls the pin and, inexplicably, tosses the grenade through the window.

"Then, without aiming, he sprays an indiscriminate burst from his machine gun into the room. The fire is returned from the inside and bullets pierce the wall and exit the exterior siding above the roof setback.

"The agent who unlimbered the first round triggers another into the room. Then, all at once, he's hit by returning fire from within. Bullets strike the back of his helmet and he falls to the roof grabbing his head. He's unhurt, but momentarily dazed.

Whitewater

"Recovering quickly, he rises to his feet and lobs the second grenade into the room. Even before the missile explodes, he triggers another burst from his machine gun that sprays bullets into the room where his three fellow ATF [Federal Alcohol, Tobacco and Firearms Bureau] agents have gone."

This bone-chilling account relates how three of Bill Clinton's Secret Service bodyguards were killed. They had been dispatched to Waco presumably to give them a rest from the "strenuous and hazardous duty" of guarding the president. These three guards were identified as Steve Willis, Todd McKeehan and Conway LeBleau. Did these three guards somehow learn something about Clinton that they shouldn't have? Were their deaths actually murders to keep them from talking? We will probably never know. But the trail of bodies doesn't end here.

On March 1, 1994, another person close to Clinton died in a mysterious plane crash. Herschel Friday was the head of Friday, Eldridge & Clark, the largest law firm in Arkansas. He crashed his private plane in Little Rock, just short of his own private airfield. His wife and son were baffled by the crash, because as an experienced pilot, Friday had landed there many times without any problems. Of interest is the fact that Friday was a member of Clinton's Campaign Finance Committee, under close scrutiny by Bob Fiske in his Whitewater investigations. Reporting on his own investigations into this and other acts of violence surrounding the Clintons, Deroy Murdock wrote:

"Can any of this be tied to the White House? Who knows? Journalists as well as investigators working for special prosecutor Kenneth Starr should move quickly to kick over the Whitewater-related rocks from the Potomac to the Ozarks and see if anything under them tries to burrow away from the sunlight.

"Also, properly handled congressional hearings would help drag all of this into the open where it can be explained as either a brutal cover-up or an interesting but irrelevant series of coincidences.

"Until then, all America can do is take President Bill Clinton at his word. As he insists, 'I haven't done anything wrong.'"

Relatively few of us know personally even one person who died in a plane crash. Most of us don't even know of someone who died in a crash. So why do the Clintons have so many close contacts with those who have met such a violent death?

The next victim is C. Victor Raiser II, who served as co-chairman of the Clinton for President National Finance Committee. On July 30, 1992, he and his son, along with three other people, were killed in a private plane crash just outside of Dillingham, Alaska. At the time of his death, Clinton's campaign was in the red to the tune of $395,000.

Mr. Carpozi mentions these deaths, which are admittedly far-fetched when trying to pin them on the Clintons. But they reflect another interesting coincidence. Five navy pilots died when their E-2C Hawkeye crashed on its return mission to their carrier on March 25,

1993. These pilots had served as Clinton's escorts aboard the *Roosevelt* during his first official function as commander-in-chief. According to the *Washington Post*, the crew had ridiculed Clinton because of his draft-dodging history.

On May 19, 1994, four Marine Corps members died when their VH-60N Blackhawk helicopter crashed along the Potomac River. Three of the members had flown with Clinton to the *Roosevelt*. Definitely a far cry from conclusive evidence, but certainly a very intriguing coincidence.

When Arkansas trooper Danny Ferguson's ex-wife died, many suspected she had been silenced because she knew too much about how he had helped the president in his womanizing escapades. Ferguson had decided to deny his role in escorting Paula Jones to Clinton's hotel room, saying that Paula, not Bill Clinton, was responsible for initiating contact. Kathy Ferguson was found dead with a shotgun blast to her mouth.

While her death was attributed to suicide, many medical examiners would suspect foul play in her case. Mr. Carpozi quotes Dr. Sydney B. Weinberg, chief medical examiner in Suffolk County on Long Island: "Women are vain. When they decide to kill themselves, they leave this planet looking as well as they can appear. They don't take their lives in the nude. They don't end it all by destroying their good looks, like blowing out their brains."

What could possibly be the motive in killing a trooper's ex-wife? Apparently, Kathy Ferguson had told co-workers at Quachita Hospital (in an interesting twist of fate, this is the same hospital where Bill Clinton's mother, Virginia Kelley, had been fired because of problems she had that resulted in more than one death), "Danny told me he solicited women by the dozens for Bill Clinton...and Paula Jones was among those women my husband told me he recruited for the governor's sexual gratification. Paula Jones has spoken the truth."

On September 6, 1986, Benjamin Paul Talbot, Sr. died in a car accident two miles out of Arkansas. On a dry road, the car ran off the highway, rolled and hit a tree. Talbot was thrown out of the car, presumably driving without his seatbelt, which his family said was completely out of character for him. Talbot ran Talbot's Department Store in Magnolia, Arkansas, and was appointed chairman of the Governor's Task Force on Small Business by Frank White during White's term as governor of Arkansas in 1982. Clinton dismantled the small business task force during his second term as governor. (The Clintons seemed to prefer large businesses, such as Tyson Foods.)

Talbot decided to campaign for White during the 1986 campaign to oust Clinton from the governor's mansion. Talbot had been on the campaign trail, speaking about how small businessmen were getting the shaft, until he was silenced forever by his fatal car crash.

Taken individually, most of these acts of violence would warrant little suspicion. If any of these deaths or fires were cold calculations on somebody's part to silence voices that had a story to tell, that somebody left little evidence that could lead to a conviction. Considering the sheer magnitude of violence surrounding the Clintons, however, it makes even the heartiest skeptic wonder if maybe an investigation isn't in order.

Another leg of the Whitewater controversy consists of Hillary's unprecedented gains in commodities trading. In her own words in the May 6, 1993 edition of the *Washington Post*, "The 1980s were about acquiring—acquiring wealth, power, privilege." Hillary got a jump on the greed of the '80s with cattle futures in what is aptly termed a "bull" market.

During a one-year period during 1978 and 1979, Hillary Clinton managed to turn a $1,000 investment into a $99,000 windfall. She mainly traded in cattle futures, but also speculated in soybeans, sugar, hogs, copper and lumber. For those unfamiliar with commodities trading, it is simply an agreement between two parties to buy or sell a certain commodity for a certain price at a future date.

Hillary opened a margin account with Refco Inc. in Springdale, Arkansas in October 1978. Her initial $1,000 investment turned into $5,300 with her first trade. Her reinvestments through the rest of 1978 resulted in $49,069 in profits, offset by $22,548 in losses, leaving a net gain for the year of $26,521. In 1979, her profits were $109,600, offset by losses of $36,600, resulting in a net gain of $73,000. Her total net gain for the ten months that she traded totaled over $99,000.

Government investigators, along with the media, raised many questions about how a commodities novice could achieve such a huge profit in such a risky venture. They couldn't see how she got away with investing only $1,000 in cattle futures, when the usual requirement is $1,200 to buy a contract, and when most firms require at least a $5,000 investment. They also had trouble believing that anybody, much less a newcomer to this legalized and incredibly risky form of gambling, could make so much money when 75% of people who invest in the commodities market lose money. It made no sense for her to close her commodities account allegedly because she was worried about the stress trading was placing on her pregnancy, and then open another account later that same year. Investigators wanted to know who, exactly, was Robert L. "Red" Bone, her main broker, and what tactics he used to gain such a high profit for her. They also wanted to know what was contained in the Madison Guaranty Savings & Loan files that were found missing by a Resolution Trust Corp. (RTC) investigator.

How she was able to get away with only investing $1,000 instead of the usual $5,000 minimum investment can be easily explained away by a broker trying to attract a powerful, if not wealthy, customer. After all, Bill Clinton did become governor of Arkansas one month after Hillary opened her commodities account at Refco, and as we saw in the Whitewater Development Corp. transactions, businessmen were ready to do anything to gain a little leverage with an up-and-coming politician. It remains unclear, however, how she managed to bypass margin requirements and buy a cattle futures contract for only $1,000 instead of $1,200. There are also questions about how she managed to satisfy state laws that require futures investors to show a minimum net income and net worth. After all, the Clintons showed few assets, and trading futures can result in substantial losses, which the trader is responsible for.

White House aides told the press that Hillary had received investment advice from Jim Blair, who was at the time outside counsel for Tyson Foods Inc., one of the companies for which she served as a board member. She also talked with others and did her own research. According to her in the *Unique Voice of Hillary Rodham Clinton*, "Jim Blair, who had been a friend of my husband's and mine for some time, talked to me about what he thought was a great investment opportunity. He is someone who has been an investor ever since he was a teenager, with usually very good results, and he had followed closely what had been happening in the cattle market. And I only knew a little bit about that, although living in Arkansas, particularly northwest Arkansas as I did, I was familiar with a lot of ranchers and people who were in the cattle industry. And when Jim said, 'I think there's going to be a great opportunity to make money,' and explained why and asked me what I thought we could afford to invest, I told him $1,000. So I opened an account at his very strong recommendation and proceeded to trade over the next months until July."

According to Jack Sandner, chairman of the Chicago Mercantile Exchange, Hillary traded "in the biggest bull market in the history of cattle." He said that from the beginning of 1978 to the first quarter of 1979, the price doubled to 80 cents a pound. "If someone caught that trend and traded it well, they could make an extraordinary amount of money, a lot more than $100,000 on a small investment," he said in the March 30, 1994 edition of the *Wall Street Journal*.

But in her own words, Hillary admitted she knew little about commodities trading, a field which is unforgiving at best. "The idea that Mrs. Clinton could turn $1,000 into $100,000 trading a cross-section of markets such as cattle, soybeans, sugar, hogs, copper and lumber just isn't believable," said Bruce Babcock, editor of Commodity Traders Consumer Report, a Sacramento, California newsletter, and the author of several books, including *The Dow Jones Irwin Guide on Trading Systems*. "To make 100 times your money is possible, but it's difficult to understand how a newcomer could do it. I don't care who is advising her. It just isn't very likely."

Reportedly, Hillary quit trading in July of 1979 because she became pregnant. Later in that same year, however, Hillary opened a commodities account with her stockbroker, Stephens Inc. in Little Rock, which trades through ACLI International, Peavey Co. and Clayton Brokerage. Her original $5,000 investment attained $26,894 in profits, but sustained a net loss of $1,000 when she closed it in early 1980, just after she had her daughter. A minor scandal erupted in 1994 when the media discovered that Hillary had not reported her gains on their 1980 tax returns; she avoided further controversy by "voluntarily" paying the taxes and penalties -- 14 years later. Other people go to jail for the same actions.

It's not known why she would begin trading again after getting out to avoid the stress during her pregnancy. It's also not known why she would have such vastly different results with two different firms...or is it?

Let's take a look at who she was doing business with. The media cited no commodities market violations on the part of Stephens Inc. But they had plenty to say about Refco and "Red" Bone. In December 1979 (remember, Hillary opened her account in October of that year), "Red" was disciplined by the Chicago Mercantile Exchange for "serious and repeated violations of record-keeping functions, order-entry procedures, margin requirements and hedge procedures." He was also disciplined for allocating trades among investors in his branch office after determining whether the trades were profitable or not.

In 1972, Mr. Bone, then an official of Tyson Foods, along with the company, Don Tyson and other parties, was accused of manipulating the egg futures market. Their case was settled in 1977 with the Commodity Futures Trading Commission, with none of the parties admitting or denying guilt. As a result, Mr. Bone was suspended from trading for one year.

Earlier, in 1975, while the case was still in progress, Mr. Bone joined Refco to run its Springdale, Arkansas branch. In 1980, a case was filed against him for trading (quite profitably) through an associate, Roy Woods, during 1977-78, just before he began working with Hillary. In 1981, he was severely sanctioned with a fine of $100,000 for this violation of his suspension, and was again barred from trading.

According to her aides, Hillary did not know what sort of person she was dealing with. However, she obviously knew Jim Blair, who got her into commodities trading to begin with, and who apparently gave her some very good advice along the way. Interestingly enough, Jim Blair was also Mr. Bone's lawyer.

In a move to increase their popularity and save face during the Whitewater investigations, the White House announced they would provide all the information investigators needed. While this new, up-front technique increased Mr. Clinton's scores in the public opinion polls, it became clear that somehow, some records were "missing." Investigators found that records from Madison Guaranty Savings & Loan had disappeared.

In March 1992, two investigators from the Resolution Trust Corp. (an agency developed for savings and loan cleanup) visited a Little Rock warehouse used by Central Bank & Trust, the institution that succeeded Madison Guaranty. The warehouse was also shared by Madison Guaranty's law firm Mitchell, Selig, Jackson, Tucker & White (government regulators took over Madison's legal work in 1989). There, they found boxes of Madison Guaranty records in serious disarray. One investigator, Jean

Lewis, returned over a year later to find that those records had been organized and that a number of the boxes were gone. She later found that some of the records had been moved to the bank. It is possible that the missing records were destroyed after Madison Guaranty failed and was acquired by a major Clinton political fund-raiser and other investors.

It is also possible that they were destroyed later than that. Leonard Dunn headed Central Bank until April 1993. He was also the finance chairman for Bill Clinton's campaign for governor in 1990, and was appointed by Clinton to the Arkansas Industrial Development Commission. During an interview, Dunn said he didn't know what happened to the missing Madison Guaranty files. "I didn't shred or dump any records" and didn't order anybody to do so, he asserted. "What motive would I have to dump records?"

Well, since he asked...how about helping out a friend? We've already had a taste of that in these pages. Good old-fashioned, down-home Arkansas politics. "It already has been widely reported that documents were shredded at the Rose Law Firm," said Mr. Bachus, a member of the House Banking Committee. "The destruction of the warehoused documents could be part of a larger effort to protect the Clintons and to obstruct justice."

The records that the Clintons did release to investigators were somewhat incomplete. Some records indicated specific numbers of contracts traded, but some only listed a cash balance with no description of the commodity and the number of contracts. While the public was led to believe that they had released actual trading records, they were simply commodity-brokerage printouts with incomplete numbers that raised even more questions about Hillary's gains. Specifically, they brought up speculations about possible abuse on somebody's part. Whether there was abuse, and who was "most guilty" in the matter will probably always remain unclear.

The most important records for discerning possible abuse are missing; there is no record of daily trade confirmations, which would indicate possible misallocations by her broker. But a little logic and some math reveal some curious phenomena. Let's look at the numbers.

One of Mr. Bone's disciplinary proceedings was "largely related to trade allocations, whereby customers of Bone's choosing would be given the good, i.e. profitable, trades at the close of the trading day and other accounts would get the bad trades." Such allocations are hard to detect on daily trades, but are difficult to get away with on longer trades without raising all kinds of red flags. Since he had already received sanctions from the Chicago Mercantile Exchange for such activities, one has to wonder if he learned his lesson (doubtful, considering he was also sanctioned later). It is possible that he was doing a favor for someone in power, someone who might return the favor later.

Which could explain how a $1,000 investment on Hillary's part could turn into $5,300 the very next day. As the *Wall Street Journal* pointed out in the April 1, 1994 *Review & Outlook*: "We and others have been asking around for explanations of how one makes 530% in one day, given the fact that, by exchange limits, the most a cattle contract (40,000 pounds) could move during that day was 1.5 cents up or down per pound. As best we can determine, the actual movement of the most volatile cattle contract on Oct. 12 was 0.8 cents. In other words, to make $5,300, one would have needed to own about 17 contracts. A contract was worth about $22,000...a position at any one time that dwarfed the worth of a couple who had a $42,000 income the previous year and didn't even own a home. The exposure to simply one day's swing would be many times the $1,000 Mrs. Clinton had put down."

There were suspicions that these might not even have been her trades, that the incredible gains she showed were somehow allocated to her account. John Damgard, president of the Futures Industry Association, pointed out that the gains she showed "very well may apply to trades that were on for some time and were liquidated that day." A White House official reported that Hillary believed that these gains had accumulated over several days. If this is true, they were not hers, belonging to somebody who was willingly or unwillingly giving up his gain to her.

One trader, Morris Markovitz, calculated that there was a point when Hillary's account was $90,000 short of margin, and commented, "I defy you to find any other account in the country where such a tiny amount of cash was allowed to risk such massive amounts of money." Interestingly, Mr. Bone has told the press that he did not confer with her over her trades (a point on which he and the White House differ), and doesn't even recall doing them.

Another possible explanation for Hillary's extraordinary profits as a novice trader is the use of a trading strategy called a "straddle," which was used often at that time. In an editorial feature in the *Wall Street Journal* on April 7, 1994, David L. Brandon explains how straddles work. Mr. Brandon was an attorney in the Office of Chief Counsel of the Internal Revenue Service from 1983 to 1989, and served as head of that department's Commodity Industry Specialization Team. According to Mr. Brandon, "Straddles have the unique ability to produce exactly equal and offsetting gains and losses that can be transferred or used by the straddle trader for a variety of purposes. During the late 1970s and early 1980s, straddles were used for all kinds of illegal activities, ranging from tax evasion to money-laundering and bribes. In fact, this activity prompted a number of legal and regulatory changes by the Reagan administration to curb the abuses."

To create a straddle, an investor enters contracts to buy and sell the same commodity, resulting in any gain being offset by an equal loss on another contract. Straddles were often used to wipe out capital gains for tax purposes. In his article, Mr. Brandon gave the following example of a straddle and how it might be used:

"An investor who realized a $100,000 capital gain in the stock market might enter into a large straddle in the commodities market. When the commodity price moved, the investor would close the loss leg of the straddle and realize a $100,000 loss, which offset his gain in the stock market. The investor was not required to report the unrealized $100,000 gain in the opposite leg of the straddle until that leg was closed in the following year. Typically, the investor entered into another straddle in the following year, thereby indefinitely rolling over the capital gain into subsequent years."

One way to avoid showing the capital gain at all was to create an account for a tax-exempt retirement fund and write the gain into that account. But Hillary clearly showed a large gain, so it's the other side of the equation that we're concerned with here. According to Mr. Brandon, people often used straddles to make illicit payments to another party. "A party desiring to transfer cash to another's personal account for legal or illegal purposes could enter into a straddle in a particularly volatile commodity, such as cattle futures in the late 1970s. After gains and losses were generated in the opposite sides of the straddle, the gain side would be marked to the beneficiary's account, while the loss side would remain in the account of the contributor. The contributor might even be entitled to use the loss to offset other gains. Such a transaction would be not only well-hidden from government authorities but potentially tax-deductible."

In any case, possible crimes that were

committed here have, very conveniently, passed the statute of limitations. In addition, incomplete records make it nearly impossible to draw substantive conclusions from any investigation. We need more information about each transaction, and records from other parties who may have realized losses equal to Hillary's gains. But in Mr. Brandon's expert opinion, "From my standpoint as a former government staff attorney with extensive experience in these matters, Mrs. Clinton's windfall in the late 1970s has all the trappings of pre-arranged trades." How Hillary could not have known that she was dealing with a less-than-reputable firm is unknown. How she could be still defending it is unfathomable, considering that she served as co-counsel on one of the lawsuits against Refco after the cattle crash.

While all the questions about Hillary's trades will probably never be answered satisfactorily, it is interesting to reflect on the fact that the Clintons won the presidency partially through their rhetoric against the greed of the '80s. During the presidency, Hillary furthered her health care agenda through condemning the pharmaceutical and insurance industries for their heartless profiteering. Ellen Goodman, Anthony Lewis and Nina Totenberg have taken up arms to defend Hillary, capitalism and honest profit. In Hillary's defense against the harsh media response to her very profitable cattle trades, Ms. Goodman came out with, "The Wall Street Journal, which has criticized her as a closet socialist, now gleefully trashes her as a closet capitalist."

Whitewater

While Hillary laments the pervasive greed of the '80s (except, we might presume, her own), relatively few people in this country have a problem with making an honest buck. We just want to make sure our leaders don't leave out the "honest" part.

And then there's Mena. A small town with a population of 5,600 in a remote corner of Arkansas, Mena became infamous for the goings-on at its little airport. In an editorial feature in the April 20, 1994 edition of the *Wall Street Journal*, Edward Jay Epstein summarizes events at Mena. "First," he writes, "back in the Reagan years, there was the CIA connection. Landing strips outside of Mena were used by the Reagan administration to stage the clandestine flights to Mexico and Central American that air-dropped weapons to the Contras."

He continues, "Second, there is the cocaine connection." Pilots apparently used the return flights from Nicaragua and Mexico to smuggle over 20 tons of cocaine into Mena. Barry Seal, the most notorious of these pilots, was allowed to continue his operation as a government informant, but was later gunned down by hit men. In *Clinton Confidential*, George Carpozi, Jr. elaborates on Seal's death. He writes that after the IRS seized Seal's major assets in 1986, he was sentenced by a Lousiana court to five years probation and fined $35,000 (not bad, considering he probably made between sixty and one hundred million dollars with his smuggling operation). The judge immediately released Seal to a halfway house, where, Carpozi writes, "The terms of his release called for Seal to report each day at specified times to the halfway house. *But he was ordered to have no bodyguards or carry arms for protection.*" Carpozi continues, "Consequently, on February 19, 1986, Seal was gunned down as he arrived at his appointed hour at the halfway house, run by the Salvation Army."

Epstein cites the next Mena activity: "Third, there is the money laundering connection. The cash generated by secret arms deliveries and drug sales—reportedly $9 million a week—led to a scheme in which local businesses and Arkansas banks were used to illegally convert the proceeds into what appeared to be ordinary business transactions. This, in turn, led to an Internal Revenue Service investigation of the companies involved."

"Fourth," Epstein goes on to say, "there is the coverup connection." He notes that the Reagan and Bush Justice Departments never brought these proceedings to a grand jury. He dismisses the fact that then Governor Clinton, too, failed to launch an investigation. In their May 3, 1994 response to Epstein's article, CBS News Correspondent Bill Plante and CBS News Producer Michael Singer point out that "Mr. Epstein says that no one is claiming that Mr. Clinton blocked legal proceedings in this matter. But as the CBS News story [two segments of "Eye on America"] revealed, Mr. Clinton was asked by a state prosecutor for help to pursue the case against Seal's associates. Help was promised but never arrived." In the segments of CBS's "Eye of America," Arkansas Deputy Prosecutor Charles Black states that Governor

Clinton promised him $25,000 to fund a grand jury investigation, but never coughed up the money. They point out that "Arkansas Rep. Bill Alexander tried to save and then re-start an investigation of Mena. Mr. Clinton did not seize on this issue and offer support, despite the fact that a Republican administration was apparently sponsoring a Contra aid operation in his state and protecting a smuggling ring that flew tons of cocaine through Arkansas."

There is no doubt Clinton knew about the illegal operations seeking refuge in his state. Arkansas state police began investigating Mena in 1984, and Clinton admitted knowledge of the activities in 1988. So why the cover-up on his part, when he seemingly stood to benefit from airing the other side's dirty laundry?

In their book, *Compromised: Clinton, Bush and the CIA*, Terry Reed and John Cummings claim that Clinton himself has something to hide. Mr. Reed, a contract agent for the CIA who trained Contra pilots at Mena, writes that he attended a secret meeting at Camp Robinson, Arkansas with Governor Clinton, Lieutenant Colonel Oliver North (the overseer of the arms operation), William Barr (future Attorney General) and various members of the CIA. Clinton himself had something to gain by mutely participating in one of this country's greatest cover-ups. In the November 1992 edition of *Criminal Politics*, founder and publisher Lawrence Patterson takes the whole Mena affair one step further, suggesting that the presidency was a payoff to Bill Clinton, and that he and Hillary "will follow the orders of the conspiracy to stay in office."

In his article, "Mysterious Mena" in the June 29, 1994 edition of the *Wall Street Journal*, Micah Morrison points out another reason for the Clintons to keep their lips sealed on the Mena affair. He writes, "There is even one public plea that Special Counsel Robert Fiske should investigate possible links between Mena and the savings-and-loan association involved in Whitewater. The plea was sounded by the Arkansas Committee, a left-leaning group of former University of Arkansas students who have carefully tracked the Mena affair for years."

Notes on Chapter 6

Page 91. Osborne, Claire G., ed. *The Unique Voice of Hillary Rodham Clinton: A Portrait in Her Own Words*, New York: Avon Books, 1997.

Page 93. Oakley, Meredith L. *On the Make: The Rise of Bill Clinton*, Washington, D.C.: Regnery Publishing, 1994.

Page 94. Oakley, Meredith L. *On the Make*.

Page 96. Stewart, James B. *Blood Sport: The President and His Adversaries*, New York: Simon & Schuster, 1996.

Page 97. Stewart, James B. *Blood Sport*.

Page 97. Watson, Kevin H. *The Clinton Record: Everything Bill and Hillary Want You to Forget!* Bellevue, Washington: Merril Press, 1996.

Page 98. *Washington Post*.

Page 99. Watson, Kevin H. *The Clinton Record*.

Page 99. Carpozi, George, Jr. *Clinton Confidential: The Climb to Power*.

Page 100. Carpozi, George, Jr. *Clinton Confidential*.

Page 102. Carpozi, George, Jr. *Clinton Confidential*.

Page 103. Gerth, Jeff. "Clintons Joined S&L Operator in an Ozark Real Estate Venture," *New York Times*, March 8, 1992.

Page 103. *The Wall Street Journal*.

Page 104. *Los Angeles Times*.

Page 104. *Washington Post*.

Page 105. *Los Angeles Times*.

Page 106. *The Wall Street Journal*.

Page 107. Carpozi, George, Jr. *Clinton Confidential*.

Page 107. Davis, L.J. "An Arkansas Thriller: The Name of Rose," *New Republic*, April 4, 1994.

Page 109. *New York Post.*

Page 109. Hubbell, Webb. *Friends in High Places: Our Journey from Little Rock to Washington, D.C.,* New York, William Morrow & Company, 1997.

Page 110. Hubbell, Webb. *Friends in High Places.*

Page 111. Hubbell, Webb. *Friends in High Places.*

Page 112. Watson, Kevin H. *The Clinton Record.*

Page 113. Carpozi, George, Jr. *Clinton Confidential.*

Page 114. Carpozi, George, Jr. *Clinton Confidential.*

Page 115. Murdock, Deroy.

Page 116. Carpozi, George, Jr. *Clinton Confidential.*

Page 117. *Washington Post.*

Page 117. Carpozi, George, Jr. *Clinton Confidential.*

Page 119. *Washington Post*, May 6, 1993.

Page 121. Osborne, Claire G., ed. *The Unique Voice of Hillary Rodham Clinton.*

Page 122. *Wall Street Journal*, March 30, 1994.

Page 127. *Wall Street Journal*, April 1, 1994.

Page 128. *Wall Street Journal*, April 7, 1994.

Page 129. *Wall Street Journal*, April 7, 1994.

Page 130. *Wall Street Journal*, April 7, 1994.

Page 131. Epstein, Edward Jay. *Wall Street Journal*, April 20, 1994.

Page 131. Carpozi, George, Jr. *Clinton Confidential.*

Page 132. Carpozi, George, Jr. *Clinton Confidential.*

Page 132. Epstein, Edward Jay. *Wall Street Journal.*

Page 132. "Eye of America." *CBS.*

Page 133. Reed, Terry and John Cummings. *Compromised: Clinton, Bush and the CIA.*

Page 133. Patterson, Lawrence. *Criminal Politics*, November 1992.

Page 134. Morrison, Micah. "Mysterious Mena." *Wall Street Journal*, June 29, 1994.

7
Scandals Galore

Hillary played a major role in appointing friends to key posts in the White House, and, from the evidence available, her tactics have not always been on the up and up. In his book, *The Clinton Record*, author Kevin Watson notes that several employees from the White House Travel Office were improperly dismissed on trumped up charges of financial mismanagement. The White House brought in the IRS and the FBI to help conduct the smear campaign against these non-partisan civil servants. While Hillary claimed to have no involvement in this matter, two White House aides said that she had directed swift action to remove the Travel Office staff.

What could possibly be her reason? It seems to be a running theme throughout the Clintons' presidency: friends helping friends while somebody else catches the heat. "The motive for firing the staff," Mr. Watson writes, "was to allow the Clintons to bring in friends who ran a private company to conduct this business. Hillary was implicated in a memo written by then-White House aide, David Watkins. Luckily, the Travel Office staff was able to fight off the phony charges and successfully defended themselves in court against the government's charges. Four White House staff members involved in the plot against the Travel Office staff were reprimanded for their actions. They took the fall and Hillary was able to avoid closer scrutiny." The job of making travel arrangements was given to a 25-year-old cousin of the president, via a for-profit Little Rock travel agency.

In *Boy Clinton*, R. Emmett Tyrrell relates the sad and painful consequences of Travelgate on the head of the White House travel office, Billy Dale: "After he and other travel office employees were fired in a plot to turn the office into a source of traditional Arkansas patronage, Dale was prosecuted. Soon the nature of the scandal and Rodham's role behind the scenes was revealed (first by David Brock in the June 1994 *American Spectator*, later in congressional hearings, and later still in the general press), but Dale had been chosen as a scapegoat and he had to spend the better part of three years and hundreds of thousands of dollars to gain acquittal while the Clintons went along with the travesty."

Scandals Galore

Hillary stirred up a comparatively mild controversy in an effort at helping children, ironically the topic she has been most applauded for. Marriane Jennings, professor of legal and ethical studies at Arizona State University, bemoans the commercial side of voluntarism hyped up by Colin Powell and entertainment celebrities such as Wynona Judd and Michael Bolton at Hillary's urging during a Philadelphia conference. To set an example for the rest of the nation, Hillary decided to visit the pediatrics ward at the Georgetown University Medical Center. "When the White House advance team saw the pediatrics ward, they were horrified," writes Ms. Jennings. "There were sick children there, many of them terminally ill. The advance team issued its orders: no children for the Clinton visit and photo who were 'drowsy, bald, bearing tubes in their bodies, or sick looking.'" Jennings goes on to note that this came from "the same woman who was bragging (pre-election) about her desire to adopt a special-needs child."

What made the photo really special was the fact that "the children in the pictures were not patients at all; they were the children of the hospital staff." A typical Clinton maneuver, really. If reality is too ugly, cover it up with a pretty picture.

And if reality is too expensive, try catering (literally) to the "big moneyed interests" you denounce in your election campaign. The nation was scandalized when it was revealed that the Clintons were renting out the Lincoln Bedroom and, better yet, were basically charging tens of thousands of dollars for the privilege of sipping coffee with Bill in the Map Room.

A Clinton memo released on February 25, 1997 from the files of former White House Deputy Chief of Staff Harold M. Ickes showed that various top donors to the Clinton-Gore campaign were rewarded with meals, coffees, golf outings and morning jogs with Bill, along with overnights in the Lincoln Bedroom. As noted in the February 26, 1997 edition of the *New York Times*, the memo stated, "Yes pursue all 3 and promptly. And get other names at 100,000 or more, 50,000 or more. cc: H. Ickes, L. Panetta, B. Webster. Ready to start overnights right away. Give me the top 10 list back, along w/the 100, 50,000."

All told, 938 guests stayed in the Lincoln and Queen's Bedrooms during the 1996 election campaign. Clinton told reporters, "I didn't have any strangers here." Of course, people who donate a hundred thousand dollars to a campaign could hardly be called strangers. As reported in the February 26, 1997 editions of *The Washington Times* and *The Washington Post*, the illustrious guest list included 370 Arkansas friends, 155 long-time friends, 111 general friends and supporters, 67 show biz friends, 128 dignitary friends and 107 relatives and friends of Chelsea. At least one third of the Clintons' guests gave money to the Clinton-Gore campaign or to the Democratic party, totalling a whopping 10.2 million dollars.

The Clintons had to give some of that money back. Johnny Chung gave $366,000 to the

Scandals Galore

Democrats and got to visit the White House forty-nine times. A National Securtiy Council official said Chung was simply using his clout with the Clintons to impress his Chinese business associates. Nonetheless, the Democrats had to return the money because it just didn't look kosher for a campaign to accept foreign monies—just slightly on the wrong side of the law.

Also against the law is soliciting campaign contributions from the White House. Vice President Al Gore was brought to task for using a White House telephone for fund-raising purposes. He basically got himself "off-the-hook" with the lame excuse that he was using a Democratic credit card.

In another exemplary performance of doublespeak, Clinton aides insisted that while Hillary's Chief of Staff Margaret Williams "took" a check on the White House premises, she didn't "accept" or "receive" it.

It may be perfectly obvious to the Clintons that they did not use the White House for soliciting campaign contributions, but they will be explaining that to the hearing committees for a long time to come.

And, of course, no recitation of Hillary's handling of Bill's scandals would be complete without a nod to Paula Jones, Linda Tripp and Monica Lewinsky.

Hillary Rodham Clinton has made clear that she sees a broad array of detractors — right-wing conspirators, partisan prosecutors and the press — combining to undermine the White House with all this attention to Whitewater and Bill's sexual harassment problems. The degree

143

to which she can be mesmerized by the press is shown in an episode from early 1996, when the first lady tried to strike back against what she saw as unfair coverage, ranging from Whitewater to Paula Jones.

The first lady reportedly ordered White House lawyers to prepare a study criticizing the work of Susan Schmidt, the Washington Post's lead Whitewater reporter. Hillary wanted their report released by the White House as a public document, but after hot internal debate other officials managed to keep it confidential.

As independent counsel Kenneth W. Starr's investigation branched out into sex and perjury allegations against the president, the White House received suggestions from Sidney Blumenthal, then a writer for the *New Yorker* magazine, that keeping track of the media might be a good idea. He is now an assistant to President Clinton whose duties include monitoring media coverage. Hmmm...

Blumenthal insists that he didn't tell Hillary that the report ought to be written, saying his conversations with her are private. Hmmm...

Blumenthal's administration colleagues call him "G.K." for "Grassy Knoll" because of his fondness for conspiracy theories. We can probably thank him for Hillary's impassioned denunciation of the "right wing conspiracy" against the Clinton White House.

Anyway, after the report was compiled at taxpayer expense, it was killed by White House press secretary Michael McCurry and Mark

Scandals Galore

Fabiani, who was then a White House special counsel.

According to the *Washington Post*, "The issue came to a head at a staff meeting in the first lady's conference room in the Old Executive Office Building."

McCurry told the meeting, "This is the dumbest idea I've ever heard in my life. I make these decisions. This is not happening." They scrapped all copies of the report.

David E. Kendall, the president's personal attorney, helped author David Brock research an article on independent counsel Kenneth W. Starr's Whitewater probe for *Esquire* magazine, hoping for a sympathetic story. Kendall gave Brock a confidential 1995 letter he wrote to the editor of the *New York Times*, complaining about a dispute he had with Jeff Gerth, the *Times* reporter who broke the original Whitewater story in 1992. *The Times* dismissed the complaint as groundless.

White House help for Brock is one of those great ironies of fate. It was Brock who wrote the December 1993 article for the *American Spectator* quoting several Arkansas state troopers as saying that Clinton had used them to arrange liaisons with women. That article, which mentioned "Paula," led to Jones's sexual harassment lawsuit against the president.

The right of Paula Jones to bring a lawsuit against a sitting president was challenged by Bill Clinton's lawyers and taken all the way to the Supreme Court. The Court ruled that Bill could carry out his duties as President while dealing with the lawsuit, so it could go ahead.

SHE TOOK A VILLAGE

The American public seemed uncon-
cerned about Bill Clinton's private life, because
they re-elected him after the Jones charges
emerged. But Paula Jones made headlines and
history by forcing President Bill to give his
deposition to her lawyers. And even more sen-
sational, Paula Jones brought former presidential intern Monica Lewinsky into the picture in
such a way that the President could find himself caught by special prosecutor Kenneth Starr
for perjury — something that could possibly
lead to his impeachment.

Jones's lawyers were interested in other
women who may have had sexual encounters
with Clinton to prove a pattern of behavior that
could help prove that he crudely propositioned
their client when he was governor of Arkansas
in 1991. Jones's story is that Clinton got her in
a room alone, pulled his penis out of his pants
and said, "Kiss it." The story brought mostly
yawns from the public.

I happened to be in the Shoreham Hotel
lobby when a flock of reporters came dashing
down the hall from a session of the 1994 Conservative Political Action Conference, spon-
sored by the American Conservative Union, of
which I am a board member. The reporters
were following Paula Jones, who had just told
her story publicly for the first time.

I was again in Washington about the time
that allegations emerged that Monica Lewinsky
had a sexual relationship with Bill Clinton.
This time I was attending to a federal lawsuit I
had brought against the president for campaign
law violations.

146

Scandals Galore

The flap over Lewinski was important mostly for its potential criminal repercussions. Paula Jones's lawyers used one of Monica Lewinsky's personal friends, Linda Tripp, who had worked with her at the Pentagon, as a source of information to ask Clinton precise questions about Lewinsky and his ties to her. They met with Tripp the night before Clinton was to give his deposition and got a great deal of information. Instead of merely inquiring whether he had a relationship with her, the Jones lawyers were able to ask Clinton about gifts and visits and other details intended to pin him down.

Although he acknowledged giving Lewinsky small gifts, Clinton denied under oath that day that he had sexual relations with Lewinsky, and said he could not recall ever being alone with the former White House aide except perhaps briefly when she dropped off papers. Again, the public took this look into his personal life as the subject for bathroom jokes, such as, "Is oral sex really sex?" Clinton's popularity ratings skyrocketed to the highest level ever.

But those statements have put Clinton in potential legal jeopardy. He could face a possible perjury charge if independent counsel Kenneth W. Starr can prove that the president had sex or was ever alone with Lewinsky for any length of time and lied about it.

Hillary's response was to circle the wagons and lash out with her "right wing conspiracy" theory. She has obviously learned what works.

147

Notes on Chapter 7

Page 139. Watson, Kevin H. *The Clinton Record: Everything Bill and Hillary Want You to Forget!* Bellevue, Washington: Merril Press, 1996.

Page 140. Watson, Kevin H. *The Clinton Record.*

Page 140. Tyrrell, R. Emmett, Jr. *Boy Clinton: The Political Biography,* Washington, D.C.: Regnery Publishing, Inc., 1996.

Page 142. *New York Times,* February 25, 1997.

Page 142. *The Washington Times,* February 26, 1997.

Page 142. *The Washington Post,* February 26, 1997.

Page 145. Kurtz, Howard. "First Lady Ordered 1996 Critique of Coverage - After Heated Debate, Lawyers' Analysis of a Post Reporter's Work Was Kept Confidential," *The Washington Post,* February 14, 1998, p. A21.

Page 146. Baker, Peter. "Linda Tripp Briefed Jones Team on Tapes - Meeting Occurred Before Clinton Deposition," *The Washington Post,* February 14, 1998, p. A1.

8
Wreckage

As noted in Hillary's book, *It Takes a Village,* "The best tool you can give a child is a shovel." From the looks of things, we're gonna need that shovel! It has already taken years for investigators to even begin sorting through the Whitewater mess, much less the new controversies that continue to pop up around the Clintons. They were able to stonewall their way through inquiries long enough to get them through the 1996 election, first denying any wrongdoing, then promising complete cooperation, then frustrating every attempt to get at the heart of the matter.

The Clintons' decision for the appointment of an independent counsel successfully deterred investigations by the media and Congress, since the grand juries convened in Little Rock and Washington made it difficult for inquiring minds to get to key witnesses. David Hale, the owner of Capital Management Services, who had originally been cooperative in various inquiries, was put in an FBI protection program, effectively removing him from the public eye.

While Bernard Nussbaum had been against the idea of calling for an independent counsel, the Clintons received a boon with appointed counsel Robert Fiske. In *Blood Sport*, James B. Stewart writes, "On June 30, 1994, Robert Fiske issued a report on the death of Vincent Foster that was welcomed by the administration; the report concluded that 'Vincent W. Foster, Jr., committed suicide by firing a bullet from a .38 caliber revolver into his mouth.'

It said the evidence 'overwhelmingly supports' a suicide, and 'there is no evidence to the contrary.'" Fiske left it at that, deciding that there was no evidence of crime to warrant a criminal probe into Foster's death. His report goes on to say, "We have learned of no instance in which Whitewater, Madison Guaranty, CMS or other possible legal matters of the Clintons were mentioned. Moreover, in the spring and summer of 1993, Whitewater and Madison Guaranty related matters were not issues of concern either within the White House or the press."

Stewart draws a shocking parallel when he comments that "while the report notes Foster's worry about the travel office affair, it glosses over what seems to have been at the heart of Foster's concern: his relationship with Hillary Clinton. The evidence suggests that Foster, a man for whom nothing 'is worth even a blemish on your reputation for intellect and integrity,' as he put it in his commencement speech, was in the process of lying under oath to protect the first lady. His situation eerily recalled that of the lieutenant commander who lies to protect his commanding officer and then commits suicide in *A Few Good Men*—the movie Foster and his wife watched just before his death."

Then Fiske was replaced by Kenneth Starr, a conservative Republican who had served in both the Reagan and Bush administrations. This replacement was the ironic outcome when Bill signed a law extending the lapsed independent counsel law. Republicans took this opportunity to call for a new independent counsel. Despite allegations by the Democrats that he was too partisan, Starr made every effort to just do his job.

And that job involved re-opening the matter of Foster's death and the circumstances surrounding it. Unlike Fiske, who did not take testimonies under oath, Starr took testimony before a grand jury.

In an unprecedent move in January 1996, Starr called Hillary Clinton before the grand jury, the first time in history a first lady had been required to do so. This stemmed from White House aide Carolyn Huber uncovering some previously "missing" records, which contradicted Clintons' story. Stewart writes,

"Though the White House insisted that the records showed that Hillary Clinton's work for Madison Guaranty had been 'minimal,' as she had consistently said, and further claimed that the records confirmed her accounts, the records in fact contradicted the first lady's sworn statement that "I don't believe I knew anything about any of these real estate parcels and projects.' On the contrary, the records showed that Hillary Clinton had billed for at least fourteen meetings or conversations about Castle Grande [a McDougal land deal], many of these with Seth Ward, Webb Hubbell's father-in-law, who was a central figure in the deal. The records show that Hillary Clinton billed Madison Guaranty for conferences on February 28, 1986, the day Ward received a $1.15 million Castle Grande loan; on April 7, when Ward received a $300,000 note; and on May 1, when Ward's option agreement—drafted by Mrs. Clinton—was approved."

Jim and Susan McDougal and Arkansas governor Jim Guy Tucker were brought to trial in April 1996 for multiple accounts of fraud in their Whitewater dealings. On May 18, Jim McDougal was convicted on eighteen felony counts, his former wife Susan was convicted of four, and Governor Jim Guy Tucker was convicted on two counts. As Stewart notes, "It was a sweeping victory for Starr. With cynicism about the jury system widespread, many had believed that no Arkansas jury would return guilty verdicts that might further the investigation of the president and first lady. But Whitewater had yielded its first convictions.

Wreckage

Then, in March 1998, Jim McDougal died "of heart failure" in solitary confinement in prison. Queen Hillary and King Bill have almost cleared the board. So many pieces have taken the fall in this treacherous game. The trail of mysterious deaths and acts of violence aside, the lives and careers of so many have been left by the wayside. The pawns have fallen like flies.

Whether by suicide or at someone else's hand, Vince Foster is dead. Whether by heart disease or otherwise, Jim McDougal is dead. Longtime Clinton friend Mack McLarty was replaced as chief of staff. Press secretary Dee Dee Myers was also replaced. Deputy Secretary of the Treasury Roger Altman was forced to resign, along with Treasury officials Jean Hanson and Joshua Steiner. Presidential counselor David Gergen left the White House, as did George Stephanopoulos and Whitewater lawyers Jane Sherbourne and Mark Fabiani. Deputy chief of staff Harold Ickes was not appointed to the chief of staff position after the election.

Hillary's Arkansas friends would have done better to stay out of Washington. Webb Hubbell pleaded guilty to income tax evasion and fraud, admitting that he had defrauded the Rose Law Firm and its clients of $390,000, and was sentenced to twenty-one months in prison. David Watkins, whose memo implicated Hillary Clinton in Travelgate, was forced to resign after using a helicopter to view golf courses for the President. Bill Kennedy resigned due to the constant pressure he received for not paying taxes for his nanny. Realtor Chris Wade pleaded guilty to two felonies and was sentenced to fifteen months in prison; he claims that business losses and attorneys' fees cost him almost one million dollars. Stewart continues the political death list: "Steve Smith, Clinton's aide in the early days as governor and McDougal's partner in the Bank of Kingston, also pleaded guilty to two felonies and agreed to cooperate. He testified briefly at the McDougal's trial. David Hale, the government's star witness at that trial, is serving his twenty-eight-month prison term. Though he is in no position to know, he told an interviewer from the *Wall Street Journal* just before the election that an indictment of Hillary Clinton was 'a certainty.'"

The end-game hasn't yet been played out, however. Kenneth Starr may yet be able to dig his way through the stalemate of denials and non-cooperation to catch the Clintons, whether in Whitewater or the sex scandals. With each denial, discovery and reluctant admission by the Clintons, they lose credence, with the public growing increasingly convinced of their complete wrong-doing in the Whitewater fiasco. How could they not have known what was happening with their money? As Stewart points out, "For reasons that seem rooted in their personalities, especially Hillary's, and in the dynamic of their marriage at the time, the Clintons seized what seemed to be opportunities to make easy money, even when that meant accepting favors or special treatment from people in businesses regulated by the state. Surely the Clintons, who went to such lengths to insulate Hillary Clinton from Rose firm income derived from state agencies, recognized the resulting

possible appearance of conflicts of interest."
With Hillary's bright mind and uncanny financial abilities, any ignorance claimed about her Whitewater investments can only be willful. Most Americans seem to know this deep in their hearts, but it is almost as if we are wishing so hard that what the Clintons say is true, that we are willing to believe it even to the point of absurdity.

How else do we explain the high public approval of Bill Clinton during the worst of the scandals?

Could the Clintons be even more right than they supposed during the 1992 elections, that character is not really an issue during this era? Will the public demand the same kind of justice of the Clintons if they are found guilty of wrongdoing in the Whitewater-Madison fiasco that forced Nixon out of the White House? We may not know the answer until well after the Clintons have finished their second term.

The clock will still be running years from now.

SHE TOOK A VILLAGE

Notes on Chapter 8

Page 145. Clinton, Hillary Rodham. *It Takes a Village and Other Lessons Children Teach Us*, New York: Simon & Schuster, 1996.

Page 146. Stewart, James B. *Blood Sport: The President and His Adversaries*, New York: Simon & Schuster, 1996.

Page 147. Stewart, James B. *Blood Sport*.
Page 149. Stewart, James B. *Blood Sport*.
Page 150. Stewart, James B. *Blood Sport*.

Bibliography

Books

Allen, Charles F. and Jonathan Portis. *The Comeback Kid: The Life and Career of Bill Clinton*, New York, Carol Publishing Group, 1992.

Bartley, Robert L., ed., with Micah Morrison and the Editorial Page staff. *Whitewater: From the Editorial Pages of The Wall Street Journal*, New York, The Wall Street Journal, 1994.

Boyd, Aaron. *First Lady: The Story of Hillary Rodham Clinton*, Greensboro, Morgan Reynolds, 1994.

Brummett, John. *High Wire: The Education of Bill Clinton*, New York, Hyperion Press, 1994.

Clinton, Hillary Rodham. *It Takes a Village and Other Lessons Children Teach Us*, New York, Simon & Schuster, 1996.

Drew, Elizabeth. *On the Edge: The Clinton Presidency*, New York, Simon & Schuster, 1994.

157

Dumas, Ernest, ed. *The Clintons of Arkansas: An Introduction by Those Who Know Them Best,* Fayetteville, Arkansas, University of Arkansas Press, 1993.

Flowers, Gennifer. *Passion and Betrayal*, Del Mar, California, Emery Dalton Books, 1995.

Gallen, David. *Bill Clinton as They Know Him: An Oral Biography*, New York, Gallen Publishing Group, 1994.

Hubbell, Webb. *Friends in High Places: Our Journey from Little Rock to Washington, D.C.,* New York, William Morrow & Company, 1997.

Kelley, Virginia Clinton. *Leading with My Heart: My Life*, New York, Simon & Schuster, 1993.

Levin, Robert E. *Bill Clinton: The Inside Story*, New York, Shapolsky Publishers, 1992.

Lewis, Charles. *The Buying of the President*, New York, Avon Books, 1996.

Marannis, David. *First in His Class: A Biography of Bill Clinton*, New York, Simon & Schuster, 1995.

Martin, Gene L. and Aaron Boyd. *Bill Clinton: President From Arkansas*, Greensboro, Tudor Publishers, 1993.

Oakley, Meredith L. *On the Make: The Rise of Bill Clinton*, Washington, D.C., Regnery Publishing, 1994.

Osborne, Claire G., ed. *The Unique Voice of Hillary Rodham Clinton: A Portrait in Her Own Words*, New York, Avon Books, 1997.

Radcliffe, Donnie. *Hillary Rodham Clinton: A First Lady for Our Time*, New York, Warner Books, 1993.

Bibliography

Stewart, James B. *Blood Sport: The President and His Adversaries*, New York, Simon & Schuster, 1996.

Stone, Deborah J. and Christopher Manion. *"Slick Willie" II: Why America Still Cannot Trust Bill Clinton*, Annapolis, Annapolis-Washington Book Publishers, 1994.

Tyrrell, R. Emmett, Jr. *Boy Clinton: The Political Biography*, Washington, D.C., Regnery Publishing, Inc., 1996.

Watson, Kevin H. *The Clinton Record: Everything Bill and Hillary Want You to Forget!* Bellevue, Washington, Merril Press, 1996.

Woodward, Bob. *The Agenda: Inside the Clinton White House*, New York, Simon & Schuster, 1994.

Woodward, Bob. *The Choice: How Clinton Won*, New York, Simon & Schuster, 1996.

Articles

Baker, Peter. "Linda Tripp Briefed Jones Team on Tapes - Meeting Occurred Before Clinton Deposition," *The Washington Post*, February 14, 1998.

Blumenthal, Sidney. "The Suicide," *The New Yorker*, August 9, 1993.

Blumstein, James F. and James Phelan. "Jamestown Seventy," *Yale Review of Law and Social Action*, Spring 1970.

Boyer, Peter J. "The Bridges of Madison Guaranty." *The New Yorker*, January 17, 1994.

Boyer, Peter J. "Life After Vince," *The New Yorker*, September 11, 1995.

Bruck, Connie. "Hillary the Pol," *The New Yorker*, May 30, 1994.

Davis, L.J. "An Arkansas Thriller: The Name of Rose," *New Republic*, April 4, 1994.

Fineman, Howard. "Big Times in Little Rock," *Newsweek*, January 24, 1994.

Fineman, Howard. "Clinton's Team: The Inner Circles," *Newsweek*, October 26, 1992.

Fiske, Robert B., Jr., Roderick C. Lankler, Mark J. Stein and Carl J. Stich, Jr. "Report of the Independent Counsel in Re Vincent W. Foster, Jr.," June 30, 1994.

Gerth, Jeff. "Clintons Joined S&L Operator in an Ozark Real Estate Venture," *New York Times*, March 8, 1992.

Gerth, Jeff, with Dean Baquet and Stephen Labaton. "Top Arkansas Lawyer Helped Hillary Turn Big Profit," *New York Times*, March 18, 1994.

Jennings, Marriane. "Philadelphia 'Volunteers' Make Mockery of Real Heroes."

Kurtz, Howard. "First Lady Ordered 1996 Critique of Coverage - After Heated Debate, Lawyers' Analysis of a Post Reporter's Work Was Kept Confidential," *The Washington Post*, February 14, 1998.

Lyons, James M., with Patten, McCarthy & Associates. "Review of Whitewater Development Company, Inc.," March 23, 1992.

Morrison, Micah. "Mysterious Mena," *Wall Street Journal*, June 29, 1994.

Pillsbury, Madison & Sutro, with Tucker Alan Inc. "Madison Guaranty Savings & Loan and Whitewater Development Company, Inc.: A Preliminary Report to the Resolution Trust Corporation," April 24, 1995.

Romano, Lois. "The Clintons' House of Cards," *Washington Post*, December 3, 1993.

Bibliography

Schneider, Howard. "Down the Whitewater Rapids: The McDougals Were on a Wild Ride, Then They Hit the Rocks," *Washington Post*, January 13, 1994.

Sherrill, Martha. "The Education of Hillary Clinton," *Washington Post*, January 11, 1993.

Sherrill, Martha. "Growing Up Hillary," Part two of three, *Washington Post*, January 20, 1993.

Sherrill, Martha. "The Rising Lawyer's Detour to Arkansas," *Washington Post*, January 12, 1993.

Sherrill, Marth. "The Retooling of the Political Wife," *Washington Post*, January 13, 1993.

Sherrill, Martha. "Hillary Clinton's Inner Politics," *Washington Post*, May 6, 1993.

Tyrrell, R. Emmett, Jr. "The Arkansas Drug Shuttle," *American Spectator*, August 1995.

Index

Index

Index

Index